For any information regarding permission

Contact: Petra Gordon via petra@petragordon.com

Book Cover design by Stonehouse Media.
Edited by Kerri-Ann Haye-Donawa.

First publication, 2020.

E-book:
ISBN 978-1-7772013-2-6

Hardcover:
ISBN 978-1-7772013-1-9

Paperback:
ISBN 978-1-7772013-0-2

This book is dedicated to a man
who changed my life,
my best friend and late husband,
IAN L. GORDON

Acknowledgements

There are many people who have supported me and encouraged me on this journey.

I want to acknowledge those who have been instrumental in supporting me in writing this book:

My late husband, Ian L. Gordon, who was my greatest supporter throughout our marriage; my mom, Sylena Clarke, who has always loved and supported me unconditionally; my sisters, Taneya Hunter and Denise Gordon, who have been there with me through every high and low, your prayers, support, and love have pushed me to write and finish this book; Vanya Caprietta, whose prayers for me helped me to finish writing when I felt stuck; one of my coaches, Nicole O. Salmon, who helped me receive greater clarity and take massive action with this book; my pastors, Apostle Bible Davids and Prophetess Rebecca Bible-Davids, whose ministry has been instrumental in my healing and growth; finally, I am grateful to God for the grace and strength He has given me.

Contents

Preface

One of the things my husband and I discussed when he was alive was becoming authors. We had walked through various challenges and believed that our stories and lived experiences would, in some way, help others. We never fulfilled that dream while he was still alive. However, it was his sudden and unexpected death that pushed me to write this book. After his passing, I felt God giving me a consistent nudge each day to write. As the days went by, the feeling intensified, and I couldn't shake it. It felt as though God had impregnated me with this book, and I couldn't rest until I put everything that was inside of my heart, spirit, and mind on paper. I truly believe God put this book in my spirit not only to help others who have faced similar tragedies and challenges, but also for my own healing.

It was very important for me to complete the writing of this book prior to turning forty. I'm happy to say that I was able to accomplish that goal. This was not an easy book to write. As I wrote certain sections, I was taken right back to the emotions of that day and those specific experiences. There were moments during my writing that tears would stream down my face. I was reliving some of the hardest moments of my life. Equally, there were moments when I was smiling from ear to ear, as I recalled the joy of the positive parts of my story. My journey will definitely evoke some strong emotions, and I suspect that those who read it will find similarities or see themselves in different parts of my story.

Through writing this book, I experienced many break-throughs specific to my mindset, forgiveness, healing, and grief around the loss of my husband and the loss of the life I once knew and lived. I completed the writing of this book the week before I turned forty. I feel as though I have closed a chapter, and I'm starting a new one. I hope the lessons I've learned will help the reader gain a greater perspective of unexpected life experiences. I felt a responsibility to pay it forward to help others avoid some of the mistakes that I have made along the way, and also to raise awareness on how to live one's best life in the face of adversity.

This book is very personal to me, as I've allowed myself to be the most vulnerable and transparent that I have ever been. I share some things in my story that I've only talked about with my husband over the years. However, including them in the book has freed me from the unnecessary pain that I've carried for years, and endured in silence. Sharing these things has instantly set me free. I pray that my story, along with the lessons I've learned, will cause you to gain perspective, and think and move with urgency as it relates to your life. Never again will I take things for granted and assume I have all the time in the world. Your entire world can change in an instant. Have faith in God. Take action, knowing that in spite of the adversity and your current circumstances, things can, and will, get better on the other side.

THE BEGINNING OF
RADICAL CHANGE

When I was a child, and someone asked me what I wanted to be when I grew up, I always replied, "A teacher." I was blessed to have some incredible teachers over the years, and I figured what better way to have a fulfilling career and life than to teach children and impact their lives the way my teachers impacted mine. That career goal changed for me in high school. One of my gifts, if you want to call it that, is my ability to actively listen to people. In general, people felt comfortable around me, even if we'd just met. It was a consistent theme, to the point where in high school, many of my peers would share their challenges with me—whether it was parent-teen conflicts, teen pregnancy, relationship issues with other friends, or relationship issues with the opposite sex. God gave me the ability to not only actively listen to people, but to also share wisdom concerning their situation. I was an adolescent who felt comfortable interacting with people older than I was, and I often helped to give counsel to them as well.

I remember the moment I started to shift my career choice. I was in my senior year of high school and questioning whether I really wanted to be a teacher. I asked myself, "If I wasn't a teacher, what would I be?" I was sharing this feeling with one of my peers at the time, and she suggested, in her very unique way of communicating, "Petra, you know everybody's business;

everybody chat dem business to you." I laughed out loud, but something about what she said stuck. It was at this moment that I started to consider Social Work as a career path. I have always loved people. I'm the type of person that would be in a line for an interview for a new grocery store opening up in the community, and have the line of people around me cracking up with all the jokes I was sharing. I absolutely love to laugh and to make others laugh, too.

I took this idea of becoming a social worker seriously, so much so that when I was in Grade 11, I applied to a summer mentorship program at the University of Toronto. Unfortunately, my guidance counsellor did not give me much encouragement, almost suggesting that the competition was too big for me to be selected. In spite of her less-than-enthusiastic response, I applied to the program and was accepted. I applied to the social work mentorship stream. There I was able to attend the Faculty of Social Work within the University of Toronto and shadow other social workers at their different jobs. It was an extraordinary experience, and I completed the program, confident that I was not only going to become a social worker, but I was also going to attend the University of Waterloo to complete my degree. So said, so done. I did exactly what I said I was going to do. I was accepted to all of the three universities I applied to and went to my number-one choice—the University of Waterloo. I completed my undergraduate degree in Social Development Studies, a four-year program, and then followed up with the completion of my Bachelor of Social Work degree, their twelve-month program.

I was excited when I graduated from university, because I was passionate about helping people and really impacting the world. I was that kid in school that hated to see the underdog mistreated. I couldn't see injustice and cruelty and just say nothing. Sometimes that got me into trouble, fighting battles that weren't mine. A strong desire to see people thrive has always been a part of me.

One of the things I was very aware of, as it pertains to postsecondary education, was how difficult it was for some who had graduated from postsecondary education to find jobs. The possibility that, after spending all that money on an education, I could end up not working in my field, but rather working at a fast food restaurant or department store, was always in the back of my mind, and it was disheartening. The truth was, there were many graduates who weren't working in their fields, and I vowed that I would not allow that to be me.

My first job in social work was not necessarily my dream job, but it's where I did my student practicum for my Bachelor of Social Work degree. I worked in the Violence Against Women sector for four years. I can honestly say it was one of the most rewarding jobs I have ever done. It was a hard job, in that these women's stories broke my heart. I couldn't imagine the level of abuse and maltreatment they suffered. I remember one incident in particular, in which a female client shared with me her story of abuse. It was common for my clients to give me the details of their story, so I could advocate on their behalf to receive priority housing. During our session, I made all the gestures of active listening. I was empathetic and kind. I was very grateful that she trusted me enough to relive her story by sharing with me. As soon as she left my office, I closed the door behind her and began to cry. The graphic details she shared of the torture and abuse she had endured at the hands of someone who was supposed to love her broke my heart. One of the things I used to say to my team, as I shared about what it meant to me to work there, was that the job was ministry for me, and the fact that I got paid was a bonus.

Overtime, I started to outgrow the organization and the role itself. I was no longer learning anything new, and that became a challenge for me. I had a decision to make: either stay in a place of comfort and familiarity, or make a move and start from square one somewhere else. I chose option two. I decided that there was more that I wanted to experience, and I needed to keep growing. I find that when I'm not being challenged to grow, I get bored, and then I get disconnected. I recognized the signs, and I resigned. I knew I would miss my colleagues, because they were amazing, but I had outgrown the place.

You would have thought that I had had enough of maltreatment and abuse through my work in the Violence Against Women sector. I ended up being hired at a Child Protection Agency. There was much excitement when I was in that interview, because I approached interviews with confidence, knowing that I had something of value to bring to the table. My perspective was that they weren't only looking at why they should hire me, but I was also assessing why I should join their organization. This is a lesson that I want to share with you: Know your value. I have often seen people fail at interviews because they lack confidence. They go into interviews from a position of desperation rather than one of posture. I always go in from a position of posture, and every job that I truly wanted I have gotten. This job interview was no different. I spent ten years in total in Child Protection Services. Something began to happen as the years went by. By 2010, I was starting to feel burnt out, and I didn't quite know what to do about it. I contemplated other jobs but didn't know another job that would give me the flexibility that I had within this organization. I knew I had to make a change. I could either change positions or leave. I eventually changed positions, thinking that things would get better. However, that thought was short lived, as things didn't get better for me. I was not as happy. I started to become negative when, usually, I was the positive, upbeat one. I started to see myself changing. I complained all the time about the job, mainly to my husband and close friends.

I was out for lunch one day with one of my friends, complaining about the job, when she asked me a very serious question. She brought to my attention that each time we got together, I complained about my job, but I hadn't done anything about it. She asked me, "Why don't you do something about it?" Her questions and bringing this to my attention hit me hard, and I started to ponder the possibility of changing my circumstance. Meanwhile, my husband was also looking into ways to help me, as he, too, was getting tired of hearing my complaints.

I owe my entrepreneurial awakening to my husband, Ian L. Gordon. He was someone that I would constantly talk to about my displeasure and unhappiness concerning my job. One evening, he invited me to a seminar in Toronto called "GAME CHANGER." If I am to be honest, I had had a long day at work in the west end of the city, and the thought of having to travel to Toronto was not appealing. That being said, I knew that my husband would be disappointed if I bailed on him, especially since I spent so much time complaining about my need for change. That night, I pushed myself to go, and the seminar radically changed the course of my life. It was the beginning of my shift towards creating something that would allow me to leave my full-time job. I was ignited during that seminar, and I enrolled in the sixty-day coaching program. Most people that were in my coaching group had an idea of the type of business they desired to build. Only one other person and I were still not sure. During that program, I was thinking about becoming a marriage consultant. However, as time went on, I realized that, as much as I loved my husband, that was not the focus I wanted my business to have.

In 2016, I was fired up about creating an entrepreneurial opportunity that would allow me to replace my income. I started my journey by partnering with a network marketing company. I was moved and inspired when I listened to how a top earner in the company, who had a counselling and social work background like me, literally took the jump from her career and was able to create success in her network marketing business. I joined that day. I had never done anything like that before. In fact, I didn't really believe in entrepreneurship. I didn't grow up with examples around me. The examples I had were all middle-class, hard-working professionals. At no time did I entertain the possibility of becoming a full-time entrepreneur some day. My husband, on the other hand, had entrepreneurship in his DNA. For as long as I've known him, that has been a passion of his. The challenge was that although he had many incredible ideas, training, and knowledge, he wasn't able to translate any of them into a profitable business. That was part of my reluctance as well. I couldn't see entrepreneurship as a viable option, because I had no personal relationship with anyone doing it and having success.

I partnered with the network marketing company for eleven months and learned a lot in terms of social media marketing and how to build your network marketing business online, without being "spammy." I invested in valuable courses that taught me about Attraction Marketing and how to brand yourself versus branding your products and services. During this time, I also invested in coaches to help me develop my coaching business, so that I could replace my income at my job and leave. It was during this time that *Radical Change* was born. I referred to my business as Radical Change because it was so drastically different from my background of social work. It was something I had not planned to do. It was completely different and literally an out-of-my-comfort-zone type of experience. Yet change on this level excited me. I developed meaningful connections and relationships through my time in network marketing. I also learned a lot in terms of skills and mindset development.

I think it's important to note that what initially motivated me to start a business was a strong desire to leave my full-time job and to build a business that could replace that income. My corporate job paid me well, with great benefits. I had become accustomed to a certain lifestyle. So I knew that in order to maintain that lifestyle, or even attain a better one, I would have to make my business work. The truth is, overtime, I discovered that creating success in business did not happen overnight, nor was it for the faint of heart. You will discover that family and friends are not your ideal clients, and that the support that you receive comes more from strangers than from those you know.

I ended up leaving that first company, as they focused heavily on branding the company more than branding themselves. In December of that same year, I partnered with another network marketing company, still in the health and wellness industry. This company was more aligned with how I wanted to build my business online. I made some incredible relationships through this company. Ideally, at this point, I wanted to generate some residual income that would allow me to replace the income of my full-time job and allow me to do what I really wanted to do, which was coaching. I think it's important to note here that at the time when I partnered with this new company, I was on the picket line at my full-time corporate job. Oftentimes, people turn their noses up at the idea of entrepreneurship because they believe their job offers job security. However, I learned firsthand that there is no such thing as job security. There were talks at the office about the staff going on strike, but never in a million years did I actually believe it was going to happen.

I remember it as clear as yesterday that on September 18, 2016 we were notified that our union and employer were not able to come to an agreement, and we were going on strike. I had never in my life experienced anything like that before. Being on strike meant that we would not receive our regular bi-weekly salary, nor would we receive any benefits. Can you imagine the impact this had on families with young children, as well employees that were receiving benefits to treat an illness? So there I was, day after day, continuing to do my live videos as I walked the picket line. I refused to allow this circumstance to rob me of my joy and my desire to build a business that would replace my income and provide me with more choices, time, and freedom. We showed up Monday to Friday and would picket, regardless of the weather—sunshine or rain, it didn't matter, we were out there. Obviously, this situation had an impact on my family financially, as bills had to be paid late. Conversations with service providers had to take place. My husband made a great salary, but that was allocated to paying the mortgage, since missing a mortgage payment was not an option. This situation went on for three months. Then, finally, just before Christmas, the strike ended. I learned the hard, but valuable, lesson that having only one stream of income was not smart. The resolve to create multiple streams of income grew even stronger for me. In fact, that experience on the picket line strengthened my resolve to leave that job and organization, and start something new. At the time, I had been working there for ten years, giving of my service faithfully. Therefore, having to go through that strike was very disheartening. It just pushed me more to take ownership of how I made money, and how I used my time. It was during that time, on December 2, 2016, that I connected with my new business partner and joined that new network marketing business.

I have been on this entrepreneurial journey for a total of four years, and I have grown and evolved a lot. I have definitely made a ton of mistakes. However, in spite of it all, I have never been deterred from wanting to pursue my business. I wholeheartedly believe that every person should have a second stream of income. I want to dedicate the remainder of this chapter to the things I have learned about starting a business that I hope will be helpful to those of you who either want to start a business or who have been grinding at your own business for awhile, without seeing the fruits of your labour.

Quitting cold turkey: I was very fortunate that when I resigned from my full-time job I had a very supportive husband who was working full-time and making a great income to hold us over while I worked on building my business. However, in hindsight, if I had to do it over, I would have secured another job that was less stressful, take a pay cut, and do that while I build my business on the side. I would ensure that I had at least six months worth of savings, and that my business was bringing in regular income for at least a year.

Here is the truth, my friend: The majority of people who start businesses are not making money right away. Success, for many, does not happen right out of the gate. There is a lot of hard work involved, especially in the front end of the business.

Most don't have the discipline or the consistency to see it through until they start earning a profit. I believe that if you are planning to leave your job, you have to have a strategy in place; don't just leave without one. There was a great tip that one of my online mentors in the industry shared that really hit home. Prior to leaving your job, imagine yourself no longer working your full-time job, what would your day consist of? How would you be using your time? The truth is, many complain about their job, but what you need to do and accomplish each day is clear when you have a job. When you leave your job to become an entrepreneur, there is no one telling you what to do each day, and you can easily waste time. Before you know it, the day ends and you have accomplished nothing. That was something I struggled with for a long time after I left my job. What should my day look like? What activities should I be working on every day to achieve my goal? People don't normally think about it. I would say it takes more discipline to be self-employed than it does to work full-time for someone else. So before leaving your job, be clear in your mind what your day will look like. Visualize how you will use your time productively.

Avoid the shiny object syndrome: Many of us are guilty of this. We get so excited about a new business opportunity that we end up spending a ton of money that we don't have. We buy every book, course, and coaching program. We attend events, some free and others costly, all with the desire to consume information that we feel we must have in order to create the same success as the creators of these amazing programs and resources. What ultimately happens is you are left with courses that you never started and books that have gone unread. You might have experienced a lot of excitement at the event, but returning home brings you back to reality, and all that fire and hype from the event fades. What's worse is that you now have even less money in your bank account, and have not made back any of the money that you spent, most times on credit. Then you, your friends, and your family start to question what you are really doing. You will evolve on this journey. It may start one way and then change, which is okay. However, prior to investing in all of those resources that you likely won't use, hone in on what you really want to do. What are the resources that are most aligned with what you are trying to create? Avoid being a jack-of-all-trades and a master of none.

Chase impact, not money: Over the four years of being on this entrepreneurial journey, I have learned that the most important thing is not making money. The most important thing is making an impact that is aligned with your purpose. Many entrepreneurs start a business while still working a traditional full-time job. Their goals generally involve making some extra cash that can help with their overall household expenses. Most of the entrepreneurs that I have spoken with over the years really wanted to be able to make money to replace their full-time income so they could leave a job they no longer enjoyed. I've learned that the more you chase money, the farther away it gets from you. When you make a greater impact on the lives of others, a by-product of that will be your business making more money. The money doesn't fulfill you; it's the number of people whose lives you can help change that is the most rewarding. When I was chasing money in the beginning of my journey, I became desperate, and it was less about serving others and more about how quickly I could make money. I've learned that making money in your business doesn't happen quickly. There are skills and mindsets that you have to develop consistently in order to create success in your business over time.

Action + Consistency + Discipline = Success: I have learned much from my experiences as a network marketing professional. One of the lessons I've learned is the importance of taking consistent action. Oftentimes, when we don't see results in an area of our lives—weight loss, business, relationship—it comes back to a lack of action, consistency, and discipline. The question then has to be asked, "How much do you really want this?" The truth is that folks get caught up in scrolling through successful leaders' social media platforms. They see the after effect, but they don't understand the behind-the-scenes sacrifices that it took to create that success. Can I be honest with you? Most people stop when it gets hard, or when they learn that success doesn't happen fast. I can speak from my own experience that when I was at my heaviest—two hundred pounds—what helped me to get rid of the excess weight was consistent action and discipline, working out with my trainer and eating the right foods throughout the day. The weight didn't drop off immediately, but after five months, I had lost thirty pounds the natural way. So if you are serious about entrepreneurship, be prepared to put in the time and work. The best way is to create a system for yourself so that you will get into a rhythm of consistently doing activities daily that will push your goals forward.

Brand yourself: This was a huge lesson for me when I started in the online marketing arena. I learned that no one cares about your product. What people care about is how you can help them solve a problem. Your target audience will buy into your ability to create solutions. They won't buy from you until they begin to know, like, and trust you. In order for that to take place, your target audience has to consistently see you creating content that demonstrates who you are, what you do, and how you can help them. It's important to remain consistent when you are building your audience. If every other week you are changing your brand or business, people will get confused and will no longer want to follow you. Get clear on what you want your brand and message to be. Who do you want to help? And how do you want to help them?

Be a producer, not just a consumer: One of the challenges for many new entrepreneurs is falling into the trap of being consumers of information only. We become "information junkies." The problem with that is we get filled up with many ideas, steps, courses, books, and programs, but struggle to implement one strategy learned. A pattern develops where we continue to consume even more information, based on the fear of missing out. We spend a great deal of money on education, without seeing a return on our investment, because no action was taken. The information can only work for you when you do the work. One of the things I have learned is to not despise humble beginnings. It's not always necessary to start big; you can start small and build and grow from there.

Understand your why: This one is very important and can often be overlooked by many. It's important to get very specific about what your "why" is. Why did you start this business? It should be more than just "to make money." Of course, we all want to have profitable businesses. However, when challenges arise and things don't go the way you imagined, it's going to require a big why to keep you going. The truth is, you won't receive a lot of support or encouragement from family and friends. They will not be your customers or clients. Oftentimes, it's strangers that will support you, more so than the people whom you know. It's strangers who will watch your consistency and reach out to learn how to work with you and get the product or service you have to offer. It's important to know your why, so that when you are feeling tired and discouraged about your business, instead of throwing in the towel, you will push pass the feelings and keep going until you reach your goals. Sometimes it requires making a change to your brand or to the products or services that you are offering. What you offer in your business is less about you and more about the people you desire to help and serve. If you haven't given your why much thought, it's time you do so. If you have already identified your why, it may be time for you to revisit and assess if anything has changed.

On January 9, 2016, I started on the journey of entrepreneurship, with no business degree nor any background in business. My background is social work, but I was willing to take the leap because I desperately wanted changed. So far, it has been a journey of self-discovery, making mistakes, losing money on bad investments, failing, and learning from those failures. I would not change any of my experiences, because I have learned to look at them as opportunities for growth and learning. As you walk out this journey, you will start to learn about your areas of strength and the skills you possess and have used in your career that are transferrable to your business. I started my journey wanting to earn an income that would replace the income from my full-time job. However, I have evolved along the way and have become more concerned about serving my community in a way that will help them to change their lives to match what they have envisioned for themselves.

On September 29, 2017, I resigned from my full-time job of ten years. I decided that I was going to go into business full-time. I was grateful for the support of my husband that allowed me to do this. He earned a great income and would be okay as I worked on building the business. However, my business did not grow fast. I experienced sporadic success, nothing consistent. What I was making truly was pocket-change and could not be seriously used to manage household expenses. I struggled, as I imagine many new entrepreneurs do, with creating a work week for myself.

Even though I was not experiencing immediate success, I still knew that having an additional stream of income was necessary, that having all your eggs in one basket was not smart. I started coaching clients one-on-one, and hosting online challenges and workshops that my audience found valuable. However, even though I was starting to see some budding success, there was still something missing for me. By fall 2018, I discovered that what was missing in my business was my faith. In my desire to create a profitable business, I was compartmentalizing my life. The truth is, my faith is a big part of who I am and my brand. I decided that moving forward, my brand would be Christ-centred. Business for me truly started to move towards marketplace ministry. I was understanding that my purpose was to serve people with my business, while giving glory and acknowledgement to Jesus Christ.

Understand that your business is not about you, it's about solving a problem. What will cause you to start out is not necessarily your products or services, since you may provide something very similar to other businesses. What will cause you to have repeat business is what you bring as a personal brand. People will come back to you because of what they experienced when they came in contact with you and your business. People buy into *you*. Therefore, it's important for you to become comfortable with being yourself, allowing your community to understand who you truly are. Spend time developing your craft, skills, and knowledge, so that you can be the very best at what you do.

Entrepreneurship is definitely not easy, but it's worth it. Having an additional source of income is no longer considered optional; it's a necessity. You may love your job, and that is wonderful. Still be open to learning about different ways you can create an additional source of income. When you understand the type of lifestyle you want to live, you can start to create systems that will allow you to live that lifestyle for a lifetime.

FAITH IN THE FIRE

My dad started to display some symptoms with his muscles, and we didn't quite understand the root cause of those symptoms. This issue continued to progress, and we later learned that he had ALS, also known as Lou Gehrig's disease. ALS is a specific disease that causes the death of neurons controlling voluntary muscles. This was the most bizarre disease for my dad to have. There was no family history of it, and my dad was fairly healthy. The most he had was high cholesterol. This news was devastating to me and my entire family. We all immediately began to pray that God would reverse this terminal illness and that my dad would be restored to complete health. Years went by, and my dad's health continued to slowly decline. He moved from losing the use of one arm, to losing the use of the second arm, which eventually led to losing the use of his legs. Eventually, he was bedridden and could no longer care for himself without a full-time caregiver. He lost the ability to speak, and it was as if he was a prisoner in his own body.

I cannot begin to express how much seeing my father like that hurt me. I was married and living outside of my parents' home. My mother and brother were my dad's caregivers, and I am forever grateful to them for the love and care that they provided to my dad for nearly seven years. It was not easy for them. When I think back to the times prior to my dad's death,

I realize that I could have visited more. The truth is, it was extremely hard for me. That sounds selfish, but it was the truth. I looked at my dad, and I didn't recognize who that person was. He had changed drastically because of the disease, and it broke my heart. I knew my dad to be a strong man. He was the provider and protector of our family. To see him in that vulnerable, weakened state hurt me deeply.

One thing I loved about seeing my dad in his home during his illness was his attitude. My dad had a sense of humour, but he was more of a stern and serious man. He was the type of man that would tell you like it is. I guess I get that from my dad. What was consistent and simply remarkable was his countenance during what, undoubtedly, was the hardest thing he had ever experienced in his life. I and other visitors would go to the home to encourage my dad. Yet, the truth is, he encouraged us by being an example of true joy and light. He smiled and laughed more than I had ever seen him do during my childhood. He was literally glowing each time we visited with him. He spent time reading the Word, and I believe he was constantly praying to God in his heart. He was at peace. I remember praying to God to either heal my dad completely or take him home to Heaven. His being restricted to a bed was not living, especially for someone like my dad who was active and always on the move.

ALS is a terrible disease. It really caused me to appreciate the little things that I often took for granted. My dad could not move or speak, but his cognitive ability was intact, and he understood what everyone was saying and doing around him. This is a disease from which people can die in a matter of months. My father kept fighting for nearly seven years. My husband and I loved to travel. We often took trips using our time share, went to all-inclusive resorts, and went on cruises. Every time I went on vacation, there was always a fear in the pit of my stomach that while I was travelling, something would happen to my dad. I feared the possibility of my dad dying while I was not there. However, I continued to travel, praying that if something were to happen, I would be close to home.

In December 2016, I joined my new network marketing company and, for some reason, I felt strongly that I was supposed to go to their conference. It was bizarre, as I'm not one to travel with just anyone. I barely knew my new teammates, yet there I was getting ready to travel with them to a company conference in Houston, Texas. We flew in Friday, and I was having a blast, enjoying the weather and the positive energy and vibe with everyone that was there. On the Saturday, I enjoyed some powerful stories and training, and I felt fired up. Then I got this message: "Petra, what's going on with your dad? I heard he was in the hospital." I froze. *What is this person talking about? My dad is in the hospital?* I asked her the question, and she apologized, because she thought I knew. It turns out that as I was boarding the plane to Texas, my dad was being rushed to the emergency department at the hospital. I knew that the last thing to go for any ALS patient was the respiratory system, when breathing became difficult. I spoke with my mom and brother, feeling frantic but trying to keep calm. My brother and mom assured me that my dad was stable, and shared that that they didn't tell me sooner because they didn't want to ruin my event. I thought to myself how mad and hurt I would have been if he had died and they hadn't told me. They encouraged me to enjoy the remainder of the event. I would be flying out the next day, and would get picked up by my husband and go directly to the hospital from the airport.

That moment was my worst nightmare come true. There I was, so far away. I felt powerless. I felt helpless. All I could do was cry uncontrollably. *How could this be happening?* I had known for years that my dad had been slowly dying, but I was still holding on to the hope of his full recovery. So I stood there, streams of tears rolling down my face. What blew me away was the kindness of the women at the event, many of whom I had just met for the first time. They embraced me, encouraged me, and gave me the space to share, if and when I was comfortable.

On Sunday, we left the conference and returned to Toronto. Ian picked me up, and we drove directly to the hospital. I was able to see my dad. He could hear my voice. He was very weak, and was deteriorating. I knew in that moment that we were approaching the end. It was my dad's wish to die at home, so he was taken home the following day. I stayed over at my parent's home, and would periodically go in to check to see if my dad was still breathing. He made it through the night. The doctor shared that he gave my dad about a week to live.

I spent the next day going into my dad's room, singing to him, praying over him, and crying, all at the same time. I could see him drifting. He was there, but at the same time not really. He was slowly slipping away. How do I describe how it felt to literally watch my dad slip away? It was, by far, one of the hardest things I had to experience. As a child, I had always wished for my parents to live until they were old and grey, and for them to die together so neither would have to live without the other.

Guests came to provide support, including my church family and my in-laws. It was actually my father-in-law's birthday, and yet there he was spending it with my mom, brother, dad, and me. I will never forget the level of support that my in-laws provided to me and my family during the course of my dad's illness. While we were in the living room area talking and eating, two other church sisters, who were family friends, were with my dad. They both happened to be nurses. They called for my mom. While we were out in the living room, my dad had peacefully and quietly breathed his last breath. Some would think that it wouldn't be as hard to bear since he had been suffering for a long time and we knew that he was going to die. I can honestly say that it was just as hard. It did not lessen the blow. I watched as my dad was bagged and taken out of the home in a body bag. The experience felt so surreal. My dad was gone. I stayed with my mom that night. She and I slept in her bed, while my brother slept on the floor. We wept. Even as I write these words, tears fill my eyes, as the pain is still very real and raw for me. I had never lost someone so close to me before.

I stayed at my mom's house for a couple of days, then I eventually returned to my home and my husband. My grief came in moments. I remember one day I was getting ready to walk out the door, when I was overtaken with so much emotion. I began to cry and wail. I mean, it was a cry that came from deep in my soul. It was a sound that I have never heard come from me before. I had to release it. Once I did, I wiped my face and kept on going. I had started a new business before my dad's passing. Most people would have understood if I had taken a break and put the business on hold after this devastating loss. However, I have always been the type of person who goes against the grain. So even though I was hurting over the loss of my dad, I knew that I could not abort my dream of building a business that would create a legacy for my family.

Over the years, I have worked in the social work profession, volunteered in my church community, and have had countless conversations with people from all walks of life. A common trend I see is that when things don't go according to plan, people get easily discouraged and throw in the towel. We cannot deny the pain that we experience when we suffer a loss, especially of a loved one. What I would encourage a person who is experiencing a loss to do is this: slow down, but don't stop completely. What ends up happening when you stop completely is that it becomes very difficult to pick back up the momentum and restart. So if you need some time, take the rest you need, but just don't stop. I have learned that the purpose God has for us is bigger than just us; someone is waiting on you to fulfil your assignment, because their destiny is connected to you.

Watching my dad go through this debilitating disease taught me a few lessons that I believe can help you gain greater perspective as you develop radical faith:

Be content in every circumstance: Philippians 4:11 (NIV) says, *"I am not saying this because I am in need, for I have learned to be content whatever the circumstances."* This seems like a tall order. How could one be content when they are a prisoner in their own body? How can one be content when they are suffering with an illness, have lost a job, lost a child, lost a spouse, lost their home? Yet here Paul is sharing in this text that he has found the secret to being content in any and every situation. The answer is in Philippians 4:13 (NIV)—*"I can do all this through him who gives me strength."* My dad was able to have a glowing countenance, laugh, and smile daily, despite his circumstances, because he had this revelation. The source of his strength came from Jesus Christ. Having this revelation gave him a peace that went beyond his understanding. That's the secret—having complete faith in Jesus, *always* and in *every* situation.

Cultivate an attitude of gratitude: This is an essential life principle, because it's easy to complain and see everything in our lives that is not good as punishment. You may struggle with feelings of being unloved, or that perhaps you have done something wrong to cause so many things to be going wrong in your life. It truly takes the Spirit of God to look at what seems like a no-win situation and respond to it with thankfulness. What I have learned is the importance of having the correct perspective and response to life's many situations. Paul shared in Philippians 4:6-7 (NIV), *"Do not be anxious about anything, but in <u>every</u> situation, by prayer and petition, with <u>thanksgiving</u>, present your requests to God. And the peace of God, which transcends all understanding, will guard your hearts and your minds in Christ Jesus."* This is the secret that most don't understand—when we respond with thankfulness, God brings peace to our heart and mind. It's not logical, so we can't intellectualize the experience. Faith does not make sense. However, I have come to learn that faith in Jesus Christ works. It's so powerful that instead of complaining about all the things that aren't going right, we thank Him for all the things that are going well. My dad was not able to speak, feed himself, walk, or move. However, he could laugh, he could see and read his Bible, and he was breathing for nearly seven years after being diagnosed, before he went home to be with the Lord. It all comes down to perspective.

Appreciate the people in your life: We live life under the assumption that those we see before us today will always be there. Rarely do we entertain the mortality of those we love. So we often take people and things for granted in our lives. How do you know when you kiss your spouse, parent, or child good night that that won't be the last time? We assume that we have another day to make it right. We assume we will have time to improve on that relationship. The truth is that tomorrow is not guaranteed. So one of the lessons I have learned is not to take things for granted. Don't leave things unsaid. Avoid holding grudges. Forgive, more so for yourself than for the other person. Let your last words to people in your life be good. Life can change in an instant, and it's the worst thing to live with regret.

Be your authentic self: I spent many years living in a way that pleased others more than myself. There were things I wanted to do but didn't do them, out of fear of what people would say. During the year that my dad died of ALS, I did something that shocked many. I coloured my hair bright, hydrant red. Some might have thought, "She must be going through a lot of grief; that's why she has this crazy hair." The truth is, I've always wanted to have red hair. However, I was worried about what the conservative church community would say. I was concerned that they would think I had lost my way, and that perhaps I was no longer following Jesus. It took much courage, but I had the full support of my husband. I never felt more freedom in my life than in that moment when my hairstylist coloured my hair and I became a redhead. Colouring my hair may seem small to most, but for me it was very empowering. I was beginning the journey of truly loving and embracing myself and who God had designed me to be. It's stifling to constantly live your life to please other people. It's not the will of the Lord for us to be slaves to the opinions of others. Psalm 139:14 (NIV) says, *"I praise you because I am fearfully and wonderfully made; your works are wonderful, I know that full well."* You are God's masterpiece, regardless of your hair colour, your fashion, your weight, or your size. All these things are irrelevant, because you are loved by God. When we come into alignment with God's purpose and intent for our lives, we spend less time worrying about other people, and more time pleasing God.

Losing a parent was one of the hardest things I had to face at that time. Despite that great loss, I never lost sight, for one second, of the fact that I was called to do more than what I was doing. So it was in the same year that my dad died that I submitted my resignation from an organization that I had served in for ten years. Sometimes during what appears to be your life going up in flames, God is creating opportunities for you to grow deeper in your faith in Him. Faith is developed and cultivated right in the fire. God doesn't wait until the situation passes to use us. He will use us right in the midst of the fire. In the fire, He is pruning us and molding us. The result is our coming out stronger and even better. The process is painful, and if I could run and avoid it, I would, with no hesitation. However, to avoid it is to miss out on the opportunity for God to develop us and to reveal the greatness that exists within us, despite our circumstances.

THE LOVE STORY

I t was September 2006, and I was starting a new chapter in my life. I had just transitioned from the church community that I grew up in, which was very difficult, since that is where I developed my roots, accepted Jesus Christ into my life, and was loved and nurtured in my Christian walk. However, God spoke clearly to me that it was time to leave and help my new pastor at the time start a ministry. Leaving was out of character for me, but thank God for my parents who loved God and loved me and knew me enough to trust that if I was making this move, then it had to be because God was leading me.

I remember the weather being amazing for September, as I was still wearing summer clothes. Those were my weave-wearing days. My hair was big like Beyoncé's, which, now when I think back on it, was hilarious. I entered a Christian bookstore with the hopes of finding a gift for my brother, because his birthday was coming up at the end of September. So I was in the store, minding my own business. I heard voices behind me, but I didn't look around. To be honest, I wasn't trying to talk to anyone; I just wanted to get a gift and then head out. I didn't end up finding something for my brother, but I did end up purchasing a DVD.

In those days, MSN Messenger was a big deal. I spent far too much time on MSN, chatting away with friends near and far. The night I returned from the bookstore, I received a notification of a message from someone that I don't normally speak with. It was Ian Gordon. Ian was more of an acquaintance through mutual friends. We had a mutual friend back in 2000, but we'd never met in person. I had attended an event, and Ian was the keynote speaker; however, he and I were never formally introduced, nor did we speak. Somehow, there was a mass email sent, and I ended up saving some email addresses; Ian's appeared to be one of them. So he messaged me that night and asked, "Was that you in the bookstore?" Now, the first thing that came to my mind was that if he thought it could've been me, why didn't he approach me? I gave him a hard time about this for years. I replied to him and shared that indeed it was me. From there, we started chatting back and forth. We chatted the night away, until the wee hours of the morning.

Ian and I talked about everything that night. He, too, had recently transitioned from the church he had grown up in. It was such an invigorating and refreshing conversation. At this point in time, I was not thinking of him romantically. I thought to myself, *This is a great person to be friends with.* I was looking at him as someone who could mentor me. We chatted every day on MSN Messenger, after that all-night conversation. It was great. One day he decided to give me a call on the phone, which was surprising. There was always something daring and fun about chatting online, but once it transferred to the phone or in-person, the experience sometimes changed. We chatted, and I started to notice certain things he would say that were more endearing. When we ended our phone call, I remember hearing him say, "I'll miss you." *Now wait a minute*, I thought to myself, *friends don't tell other friends that they will miss them.* I must give a disclaimer: I'm the type of person who doesn't like to beat around the bush. I like to talk straight and tell it like it is. Sometimes it's well received, and sometimes not so much. God continues to work on me and my delivery. In this case, I was starting to sense a shift. I was starting to feel that something more than friendship was developing. I'm rarely wrong about these things, but for the sake of being sure, I decided to ask the question. What was great about this season was that our communication was not limited to just instant messenger, but we would also email each other long letters. So I emailed him one day—this was my "hotmail.com" days. In that email, I shared that I was a very transparent person and that I could be totally in left field and that if I was, we could simply carry on as friends. However, I sensed that something was developing between us that felt like more than friendship. He replied right away and confirmed that I was not in left field and that there was something developing. He suggested that we meet in person to see if what we were experiencing went beyond the computer screen.

There was a women's church event that he told me about that was taking place in the city. I went with my mom on the first night. We didn't really get the opportunity to speak. He said hello in passing and handed me a CD. My mom raised her eyebrows, and she asked, "Who was that?"

"Just a friend," I responded.

I went back the following night, this time by myself. Ian had wanted to meet me in person to talk, and he had brought his sister along. I must be honest, I chickened out. I was so nervous to meet him and his sister. Perhaps if it were just he alone. I wasn't sure what to expect, not knowing him and his sister and how that would be. So after the service, I saw him standing with his sister, and I walked behind him, unnoticed, because it was such a crowded event. Ian could not be missed in any building, because he was six-feet-one-inch tall. I hopped into my car and drove away. Immediately, as I was driving away from the building, I received a call from Ian. "Where are you?" he asked. I shared that I had left. He laughed at me, knowing I had chickened out. We agreed that we would set a date to meet in person, alone, at Denny's.

We met at Denny's. I can still remember the butterflies in my stomach, the anticipation of meeting him, hoping that this experience would be unlike every other experience. I was hoping that the chemistry I was feeling online in our conversations would transfer to our in-person interaction. We sat across from each other, and I ordered a burger and fries. I assured him that I was not a water-drinking-salad-eating kind of girl. It was a wonderful first date. We talked, laughed, and shared about life and spiritual things. It truly was a magical night, and we both immediately knew that what we had was real. We were meant for each other. I remember when we left the restaurant that the first person we called was our mutual friend, because without him, we would have never had a connection, since we didn't run in the same circles.

We continued to date and talk on the phone daily. The next step was to share with my family. Oh, my goodness, that was super awkward for me, as that was not the type of thing that I would share and talk about with my parents. However, I had to do it, because Ian did not grow up in my church, and we were not in the same church circles, so my parents and brother did not know him. I had to call a family meeting, which was weird, as we don't do family meetings. That was the only way I could get them all together to share what was happening. So I shared that I had met someone that I believed was the one. The only thing that was a bit of an issue was the fact that Ian and I did not come from the same denomination, which, in those days, was a huge thing. There were some minor differences in some of our doctrinal beliefs around baptism. In my denomination, it was frowned upon to marry someone outside your denomination. So I didn't receive much support when the word got around about my relationship.

We eventually met each other's families, which, honestly, was also very new for me. My family was already familiar with everyone I had dated previously, so it was weird for me to go through this process. However, we did it. I survived, as both families were loving and kind to each of us. We dated for a year. During that time, both our parents came together to meet and get to know each other. The biggest question that both sides had was, "How is this going to work?" Ian's parents didn't want him to stop being a part of his denomination, and my parents didn't want me to stop being a part of mine. I can laugh at this situation now, but it was a huge thing at the time. Truthfully, Ian and I didn't understand how it would all work out, as we were both ministers and very active in ministry. All we knew was that the love we shared for each other was real, and we believed that God was in our relationship, even though it didn't make sense to everyone around us.

After dating for a year, we were then engaged for a year. We got engaged a few weeks after I changed jobs and joined the organization that I worked at for ten years. We then got married in August 2008. The days leading up to my wedding day were very stressful, mainly because of the opposition of those who didn't feel I should be marrying Ian, because we were not a part of the same denomination. We both submitted our relationship to God and sought counsel from other spiritual mentors and leaders. The confirmation was consistent. However, some church members that I considered to be family did not attend my wedding. Their beliefs were so strong that they felt they could not support by attending. I was hurt by that. If they had just gotten to know Ian, they would've seen that the same Jesus that lives in us was the same Jesus living in him. I'm thankful that it was evident to my parents that Ian, indeed, was a man of God who loved Jesus. I received my parents' blessing, which was all that really mattered in my eyes.

I was nicknamed "the Preaching Bride," after my wedding speech. In fact, a clip of it can still be found on YouTube. I had planned to say nothing on that day. However, when my husband turned to me and asked if there was anything I wanted to say, I took the microphone, not realizing what was going to come out. It was such an emotional day. I just expressed my appreciation for the goodness of the Lord; after all the opposition leading up to the day, we'd made it. When I look back at the wedding video, there was not a dry eye in the house. In "Petra's fashion," the wedding was not traditional or ordinary. Instead of dancing the night away and throwing my bouquet, there was an enormous receiving line of people. There Ian and I thanked people and spoke blessings over their lives. It was one of the most powerful encounters of my life. It was just a confirmation of what our life together was going to produce. Our marriage would break barriers and walls between our denominations. We were very intentional to visit together at our former congregations to show how these two ministry expressions could come together and still serve Jesus Christ, without compromise.

The first year of marriage was very eye opening. Even though Ian and I had participated in premarital counselling, and had shared and talked about everything under the sun, I came to realize that you don't truly know someone until you live with them. You start to see the behind-the-scenes, and you must learn how to coexist and bring two completely different people and lives together to become one. It was not an easy process. I have a type A personality, I like things to be in order, and I'm a bit of a clean freak. My husband was the opposite. I would get annoyed whenever I found socks on the floor, or a messy space in general. That stuff did upset me in the first year. What I had to understand very quickly was that if I wanted my marriage to last, there were some things I had to let go of, and I had to pick my battles. I also had to understand that Ian was not me, and he was not going to do things exactly the way I did them, and I had to learn to be okay with that. It was a journey and a process of growing together, since I was no "walk in the park" either. However, God gave us the grace we needed.

One of the things that happens after a young couple gets married is that people start asking questions about having children. The questions increase as the years go by, especially when there are no children in sight. Prior to getting married, I never imagined that having children would be difficult. At no time did I entertain the possibility of complications. However, year after year, I was not pregnant. I finally decided to go to a fertility clinic and found out that I had endometriosis, which is a common condition among women that can result in infertility. So I required a minor surgery, which would make it possible for me to get pregnant.

One of the most challenging things during this time was the insensitivity of people's remarks to me, as it pertained to having children. One person passed a remark to me one day, reminding me that I'm getting older, and that I shouldn't wait any longer and risk my children having Down Syndrome. Truthfully, I should have been more upset, but I chalked it up to the person's ignorance. I remember another person jokingly telling his young son to lay hands on my stomach and repeat the word "Conceive." While others questioned if I even wanted children, and judged me unfairly, suggesting that I was more concerned about keeping my figure. During that time, I had also gained a lot of weight from not taking care of my body. I recall someone congratulating me. That would have been great, if I was actually pregnant. I told the person, "I'm not pregnant. It's just gas and fat." I also recall one person telling me that I should hurry up and give my dying father a grandchild, so he can enjoy having a grandchild before he died. The list of insensitive and hurtful things that were said to me during this time is long. Do I believe people were intentionally trying to hurt me? No, I don't. However, that doesn't change the sting of their words during a time that was extremely difficult for me.

I know that there are many singles that desire to be married, and it's a good desire. I do want to make it clear that marriage is a lot of work. It's far more than just sex and companionship. There are a lot of different challenges that you face in a marriage that you must learn to work together to get through. We see a lot of divorces today, because folks are not willing to do the work and remain together. It doesn't take much for couples these days to call it quits, which, quite frankly, I find sad. I've come to learn in my marriage that love is more than a feeling; it's a choice. I chose every day of my marriage to love my husband, and to remain in the marriage, until death do we part.

I can honestly say that the process of doing the investigative work to understand my fertility was the most intrusive experience of my life. Just imagine having to get up early in the morning and not go to the bathroom, which is what people normally do. I had to hold my urine and wait to urinate in a cup, to give a sample. I had to participate in blood work. It was a repeated process, which I did not enjoy. However, it was necessary to understand the issue I was having. My surgery was successful, and we could move forward.

It was during this time that my husband's health started to decline. He had been diagnosed with diabetes years before meeting me. Truthfully, I never thought diabetes was a big deal. My mom was diagnosed with it in her fifties, and she seemed to be doing well. What I didn't realize was that when unmanaged, it can lead to different illnesses, and, ultimately, can shut down certain organs of the body. Diabetes is not to be ignored. Any person that has it or knows someone that has it needs to strongly recommend keeping on top of the disease, so that conditions don't worsen. We live in a day and age where you can be healed from diabetes, and it does not have to result in further damage to other organs of the body. My husband had difficulty managing his diabetes. He just wasn't able to get a handle on it.

Prior to my husband's health starting to significantly decline, we enjoyed eight years of marriage. The following are some of the things that helped us to have a strong marriage, in spite of our ups and downs:

Never stop dating: One of the things I loved about my relationship with Ian was that we both loved to have fun together. We continued to date. One of our favourite things to do together was going to the movies. We also travelled several times a year, and even bought a time share to accommodate our love for travelling together. We valued quality time. Sometimes he would watch a "chick flick" with me, and I, in return, would watch a sci-fi show or superhero movie or television show with him. We would do things that the other enjoyed, because it was quality time spent together.

Laugh often: Ian and I both loved to laugh. He had one of the heartiest laughs around. It was the most contagious thing ever. Even though we faced challenges in our marriage, we kept things light. We didn't hold grudges or give each other the silent treatment. We were best friends, and we knew each other intimately. We became so in-sync over the years that it was almost as if we became the same person. I would be thinking a thought, and he would say exactly what I was thinking. I would always turn to him and ask, "Are we twins?" and then we would both laugh out loud.

Communicate about everything: My husband was more of an introvert and a deep thinker. However, he would stretch himself all the time to engage people in conversation and to move outside of his comfort zone. I also had to stretch him to talk about his feelings, and to feel safe to share his feelings, even if I didn't agree or even if it would make me upset. We shared everything. If something exciting happened, we would tell each other. If we were upset, frustrated, hurt, or disappointed, we would share it with each other. We communicated about the good, the bad, and the ugly. We had tough conversations, and we would do so in love and with patience. We weren't perfect, but we tried our best to be sensitive to each other's needs.

Make God the centre of your marriage: Ian and I were both devout Christians, and our faith in Jesus Christ was what guided us in our relationship. It was the pillar that kept us strong during testing times in our relationship. We knew that Jesus was our anchor, and that no matter what challenges life threw at us, we would get through them with the help of the Lord. Jesus was the glue in our relationship that helped us to stay strong.

Keep third parties out of your marriage: Ian and I were very intentional about not allowing any person, no matter who they were, to get between the two of us. If we had an issue with each other, we would talk to each other. We would not lean on the opposite sex for counsel. We didn't let anyone come into our relationship and pin us against each other. We were loyal to each other, and we had each other's back. We did not shame or embarrass the other publicly. We were discreet and would cover each other, always. We made an agreement before we got married that I would manage my family, and he would manage his. It's easier for our families to forgive us, because we are their blood. So that worked for us.

Understand your spouse's love language: This is a big one, because my love language was different from my husband's. However, we learned how to express love in the language that would meet each other's needs.

Don't take each other for granted: The longer you are together, the easier it is for this to happen, if you aren't intentional. That's why it's important to communicate your needs. Have couple's meetings and talk about things pertaining to sex, finances, and other needs in the relationship. Never assume. Your spouse could be thinking and feeling things that, unless you talk about them, could stay buried and could build up over time. We were very intentional about not going to bed angry.

Give each other space: When I speak of space, I'm not referring to when wives talk about needing a break from their husband. I'm speaking about moments when you are at home and you both go off to do separate things for yourselves and then come back and eat together or watch a show together. Ian and I did this naturally, without even having to say anything. It was an unspoken rule, and it worked. We would enjoy our own individual quiet time, and then we would equally enjoy our couple time.

Get on the same page when it comes to finances: One of the biggest issues that impacts marriages is finances. My husband and I took some time to get on the same page concerning money. It is not an easy thing to do, but it is totally necessary in order to build a stronger financial future for your family.

Don't stay angry: Be quick to forgive, and avoid going to bed upset with your spouse. Life is short, and no day is guaranteed. Let the last words you say to your spouse after a disagreement be "I'm sorry." One of the things I loved about Ian was that he was always quick to say sorry and mean it. I couldn't stay upset with him long, because he was so compassionate and sincere in his apology that I would be moved to forgive and let the offense go.

Marriage is a life-long commitment. One of the greatest lessons I learned about marriage was that loving each other is a choice. Undoubtedly, there will be challenges, but there will also be some incredible times; embrace all of them. Learn from every experience, and grow together. I could not have asked for a more loving and caring husband than Ian L. Gordon. He was my greatest supporter and my best friend. Ian helped me to believe in myself, when I lacked confidence. He stretched me to see that I had a capacity for entrepreneurship, before I could even see it in myself. Doing life with Ian was one of the greatest joys of my life. We made an incredible team in everything we did together. Find someone that you can build a lifetime of love and legacy with. Someone who is not afraid to dream big with you. I found that person, and he changed my life forever.

IN SICKNESS AND IN HEALTH

Diabetes is a slow killer. I truly underestimated the impact that it could have on a person's life. Perhaps it was because I saw so many examples of people being able to manage and control it. Overtime, Ian's health started to decline. Initially, it was the challenge of managing his blood sugar level. Sometimes it was too high, and other times too low. Food was a challenge as well, and we tried different methods over the years to help with his weight-loss journey. We did everything, from juice fast, Daniel fast, smoothies, vegan meals, to a naturopath supplement. All these efforts were short-lived, as they didn't turn into a lifestyle that could be maintained. Anyone that has ever been on a weight-loss journey can relate to the challenges around not only losing weight but also keeping it off. My husband and I always had the same struggle around what to cook. I was much simpler when it came to food. I could cook and eat leftovers for the entire week and be good. My husband was not a fan of leftovers, and would be bored of the meal after one day. So it was hard to figure out a diet he could be consistent with that would assist him in losing the weight.

I started to notice my husband having increasing challenges with his digestive system, which his doctor explained was a result of the diabetes. In addition, he started to experience challenges with his vision, because the diabetes had entered his eyes. The impact on his vision resulted in Ian having to receive treatment on his eyes monthly in order to bring his vision issues under control. Naturally, this concerned me, as my husband was young—he was only in his late thirties—and I wanted him to be around for a very long time. So I supported him, by going to his doctor's appointments and his eye-treatment appointments.

The next thing I started to notice was a swelling developing on his leg. I pointed it out to him and encouraged him to see his doctor to further investigate what was causing it. My husband was not a fan of going to the doctor so frequently, and he hated the fact that he had diabetes, so frequent visits to the doctor were not at the top of his priority list. However, he went. He got his bloodwork done. He had an incredible doctor that literally spoke to him as though Ian were his son.

At this point, we were down to one car, because Ian's car had shut down, and at the time it was not worth putting more money into that vehicle. Ian worked downtown Toronto and commuted by public transportation, so I started to drop him off to work in the morning and pick him up after work. I remember one evening when I picked up Ian from the GO Transit station, he shared that his doctor had called him and told him to go straight to the emergency department at the hospital. His doctor had just received the results from Ian's most recent bloodwork, and he shared that it was urgent that Ian go straight to the hospital. I stayed calm and drove him to the hospital. I would be lying if I said I was not concerned. On the surface, he didn't seem to be in pain, but whatever came up in his test results had concerned his doctor enough that he wanted Ian to go to the hospital right away. During this time, Ian's legs had continued to swell. It seemed as though he was holding in water. When we arrived at the hospital, we did what most people do when they go to the hospital, we waited. He registered, and we waited. When he finally got called in, we continued to wait all night by the nursing station. I absolutely hate being in hospitals. I hate the smell of hospitals, and I have to fight not to get nauseous and throw up. After several hours, my husband finally received a bed, and what really upset me was that the bed they had for him was right in front of the nursing desk, because there were no rooms available. There was absolutely no privacy. This is one of the other issues I have in going to the hospital. The beds are limited and, more times than not, patients are made to wait in the hallway. I was sitting on a hard and uncomfortable chair. Ian saw how much I was struggling and encouraged me to go home and return later. At this point, it was the wee hours of the morning, and there was nothing that was going to be done for Ian at that point, so I agreed to go home and return later.

I returned a few hours after leaving him. Ian was no longer in front of the nursing station, so I proceeded to ask where my husband had been taken. I finally found him again in a space that was not a room. There was a divider in a corner of the hospital, and that was where they had my husband, due to the lack of beds and rooms. I was so livid about this type of experience. I resented the fact that he had to go through that. Finally, a doctor came to see my husband while he was in this corner. He was advised by the doctor, who I later learned was a kidney specialist, that they were going to have to keep him in the hospital longer, and that there were concerns about the functioning of his kidneys. We were alarmed by this news. The kidney specialist explained that diabetes has an impact on the kidneys. He explained to us that Ian would need to start seeing him in his program to start treating his kidneys. He told us that he believed that Ian would eventually need to go on dialysis, based on the current condition of his kidneys. At the time, neither Ian nor I accepted that prognosis, and we were believing God to turn the situation around so that he would not have to be on dialysis.

Ian was finally moved into a room and spent an extra day there for them to drain some of the fluids that had built up in his body. The swelling that we were seeing in his legs was a result of his kidneys not functioning as they should. Prior to being discharged, a dietitian came to see Ian and reviewed with us what he would need to eat, and what he needed to stay away from. He would also have to attend regular appointments at the hospital to meet with the kidney specialist. During this entire time, we were praying and believing God to turn this situation around. I already knew that having diabetes was something that Ian was not pleased with, and hearing the news about his kidneys was another blow. Nevertheless, he pressed through, and was optimistic that things would turn around.

For the most part, Ian was attending his specialist appointments on his own, receiving information about dialysis and kidney donations. We both continued to maintain the stance that he would not need to undergo dialysis and that his kidneys would be healed. One day he had an appointment with his kidney specialist, and I felt an urge to go with him. I truly believe it was the Holy Spirit. Ian and I went together, and what the kidney specialist had to share was not good. He shared that, at that point, there was nothing else they could do for Ian, and that he was at the point now where he needed to go on dialysis, or else he would start to experience worse symptoms. Ian was already experiencing extreme fatigue, as the swelling of his legs persisted. The imbalance of his sugar levels continued, he wasn't feeling good, and his health was not improving on its own. A decision needed to be made. The kidney specialist advised that he could not force Ian, but also made it clear to him that there was nothing else he could do for him at the clinic. The only thing he could recommend was dialysis, and getting Ian on the kidney donors list as soon as possible. I knew Ian didn't want that, nor did I want it for him, but we were now at the point where he was feeling worse, and his kidneys needed the help. So that day in the doctor's office, we agreed that he would proceed with the dialysis, and that he would do the least intrusive treatment that would allow him to do it at home.

We left the doctor's office not pleased with the outcome, but still full of faith that God was going to turn the situation around somehow. Over time, Ian began to disclose to me some of the challenges he was having, even on his commute to work. He was carrying extra weight from all the water he was retaining. He was experiencing light-headedness more frequently, and shared with me that there were a few instances where he had fallen while at work. His balance was being affected. He fell, and thankfully there were people around to help him back up. We talked about his safety and the concern around him falling down the stairs. We decided that he would speak to his manager and request to work from home, until he got his health condition under control. Thankfully, he had a very supportive team and manager who accommodated his request to work from home.

We were in the summer months at this time, and Ian was scheduled to return to the hospital to have a procedure done to put the peritoneal dialysis catheter in. We would first attend the training, and then he would get it surgically put in. I recall that day at home—it was warm outside the house, as well as inside, since it was June 2018. Ian was not doing well. He was extremely cold, walking around with a blanket, and had a heater on in his office. We couldn't explain what was happening to him. He took frequent trips to the washroom, and he felt weak. I assisted him as he walked out of our en-suite washroom and back into our bedroom. He fell forward onto the bed. At first, I thought he was playing around, just to show me how tired he was. However, I quickly realized he was not playing. He fell forward, his eyes rolled up into his head, and he became unresponsive. It was at that moment that I began to panic. I was very scared, because I had never seen Ian that way before. I dialed 9-1-1 and spoke with the operator and explained, frantically, that my husband was unresponsive. The operator encouraged me to calm down and explain what was happening. I was calling Ian for what may have been a few seconds, but what felt like an eternity, as he wasn't responding. While on the phone, I called out his name again, and he started to move his lips and show that he was conscious. I got off the phone with the operator, after giving her our address. Ian slid off the bed to his knees. I went to his side and tried to lay him down, but that only made what he was experiencing worse, as he couldn't breathe while lying down. So I managed to lean him up against the night table until the firetruck and ambulance arrived. My husband was six-one and over two-hundred pounds, so when he fell, that was a lot of weight coming down. Thankfully, the ambulance and firefighters didn't take too long to get to our house. The firefighters were the first to arrive. Ian was not able to walk himself down the stairs, so they strapped him to a chair and carried him into the ambulance to the emergency room. After this incident, everything began to decline rapidly.

I contacted his parents immediately, to let them know what was happening. I also contacted my mom, in tears. I couldn't believe this was happening. I could have lost my husband in that moment when he fell forward and was unresponsive. However, I couldn't entertain that thought for too long. I grabbed an overnight bag and his medications, and headed to his parents' house to pick them up, along with Ian's sister, to go to the hospital.

Visiting the emergency department was starting to become a regular occurrence, which I didn't like. The smell and the sounds of other patients screaming in pain made me uncomfortable. My body was exhausted from lack of sleep and overall concern for my husband and what he was going through. Thankfully, this time around, he was given a room and a bed. We waited for what felt like hours. When I couldn't get comfortable, I ended up sleeping in my car for a bit to try to get some rest. It was such a difficult time. I would pray, and at times cry, throughout the night. I could not believe it had gotten to this point. My husband was way too young for this; he was only forty-one years old. Even at that moment, despite how bad it seemed, I still refused to believe anything less than his full recovery. I didn't know how God was going to do it, but I was believing that things would get better.

Ian remained in the hospital and was admitted to a room. "His lungs and body were filled with so much fluid that he could have died," the doctor shared when he came to see him. So he had to get the surgery right away to start the dialysis while he was still in the hospital. He successfully went through the surgery and got the catheter in. The nurses started to administer the dialysis while he was in the hospital, to start removing the build-up of fluids that was in his body and lungs. Ian had to remain in the hospital until the fluid that was filling his lungs started to go down, because it was impacting his ability to breathe comfortably. I was at the hospital every day. I took breaks to go home and shower, sleep, grab anything Ian may have needed, and then went back again. When they felt that he was stable enough to start the training for the home dialysis, he was taken to the kidney dialysis clinic, and there he and I were trained on how to administer the home dialysis.

I remember there being a lot of information; it was a huge learning curve. It was important to clean the area where the catheter was inserted, in order to avoid infection, which would be extremely painful for Ian. There were all these steps that he had to take, every morning and evening, around tracking his weight and blood pressure. It was a huge adjustment to Ian's life and ours together. Our bedroom at home was like a hospital room, because I had to set up the machine, and get all the supplies ready for his eventual return home.

After intensive training, and after the majority of the fluid had been removed from Ian's body, he was able to finally return home. It was good to have him back home, and I was extremely thankful. At that point, returning to the office for work was not an option, so he was granted further permission to work from home. I was thankful that I had resigned from my full-time job the previous year, because I wouldn't have been readily available to be there for Ian if I still had that job. He had multiple medical appointments at the hospital with his kidney specialist. Overall, we were getting the handle of home dialysis treatment. The goal was to get him on the kidney donors list. I got tested to see if I was a match. Unfortunately, our blood type was different, and I was not a match.

The magnitude of how much our lives would change began to hit me. Since Ian and I loved travelling, at one of his kidney appointments I asked how travelling would work. Ian's nurse advised that it was possible, but there would be some extra planning and preparation that would have to be done to make it possible. I remember tears starting to roll down my cheeks. This diabetes was robbing my husband and I from doing one of the things we enjoyed doing most together. I had a moment where I started to grieve the loss of things that we could no longer have or do until he got a new kidney.

I would be lying if I said it didn't feel like a heavy load. We were still young, and there was a lot that I still wanted us to do together. In spite of the weight of the doctor's reports and our new normal, I still refused to accept anything other than my husband's full recovery. At no time did I entertain anything but Ian's coming out of this stronger than ever. I truly believed that we would have a powerful testimony, and that our marriage would be even stronger as a result

Even though Ian was on dialysis for several months, it did not appear as though he was getting better. He would experience shortness of breath, and, on occasion, he would fall. As a result, I would not let him go places on his own. Activities that we used to do together, like grocery shopping and going to church, I started to do alone, because of how fatigued he would be. It didn't quite make sense to me that he was not getting better.

I started to work a relief job at a women's shelter to assist with bringing in some income. Even though Ian was still getting paid, I wanted to help, so I picked up frequent shifts, which were helpful. The majority were evening shifts, so I could be with Ian during the day and make sure he was set up at night for the dialysis. As time went on, working from home started to become difficult for Ian. He just didn't have the energy. Ian got to the point where he had to seek information on going on sick leave until he got better with a new kidney. When Ian told me that he was not able to return to work, it was a hard blow. I remember the day vividly. I was on my way to my afternoon shift at the shelter when he shared the news with me. My mind started to race, thinking about what this move would mean for us. If he was no longer working, and he had been the main bread winner since I resigned from my full-time job, I would have to return to my full-time job in order for us to manage. The application for sick leave took at least three months to process.

I didn't have enough time to process all of this information before going to work that afternoon. My colleagues were used to an upbeat, life-of-the-party Petra. However, on that day, I was lowkey and subdued. My colleague and supervisor were in the office. All my manager had to ask was, "Are you okay?" and I immediately started to cry. She encouraged me to take a moment. So I walked down the hallway of the shelter to avoid seeing any clients, tears streaming down my face. I went to the staffroom, since no one else was there, and I bawled my eyes out. I just felt as if we were being hit with one thing after another. I hated what this illness was doing to our lives, and it was unclear what the outcome would be. Nevertheless, even at this point, I was still believing God to turn this situation around. I regained my composure. I received great support from my supervisor, and I explained to her the news I had just received and that I didn't have time to process it prior to coming. She understood, and I was able to complete my shift.

I started working at that shelter in September 2018, and the Lord led me on a twenty-one-day water fast. I had never in my life gone on a water fast for that long. However, I felt strongly that God was calling me to do it. Believe it or not, I had more strength and energy than when I was eating food. I felt closer to

God and was growing in my faith. My prayer life intensified, as I would get up early every morning to pray. I thought this prayer and fasting was for my husband's complete healing, for our finances to get in order, and for our marriage to be strengthened during that time. I really didn't know what was getting ready to happen. I was not prepared for what would be the thing to rock my entire world. Life, as I knew it, was never going to be the same again.

During the time of my husband's health declining, I learned the following lessons:

Self-care is mandatory: In general, self-care is important. Even more so when you are the caregiver for a sick relative or, in my case, a spouse. I felt very much alone in this process. I felt the weight of taking care of my husband, myself, and our household all fall on me. I didn't feel I could take time for self-care. I just kept going, which was not good. It's important to take those moments. Eventually, whenever I would go grocery shopping for us, I would take an extra drive to clear my head and just take a break from this new normal. Find the thing that you can do to relax your mind, even if it's for thirty to forty-five minutes.

Patience is needed when caring for a sick relative: In general, when you are married to someone, it requires patience and understanding. When that loved one is sick, it requires even more patience and understanding. Demonstrating grace and kindness towards your loved one is key.

Develop a strong support system: I wish that I had done this. When I think back, I wish I had reached out more. I wish I could have felt comfortable to be vulnerable enough to let someone in, to share my frustrations and hurt about what was happening. However, I didn't. I turned to God alone. I didn't feel as though I could let people in. It's important to surround yourself with people you can trust, who can be a rock for you when you are feeling weak. Without a doubt, Jesus Christ is my anchor, but at the same time, He brings people into our lives that love us and want to help us. I spent so much of my life dealing with my own stuff that I truly didn't know how to let my guard down and show what seemed to me to be weakness and vulnerability. I kept powering through. Lean on the people who genuinely love you.

Your love is tested when a loved one gets sick: I always knew that I loved my husband. Not only did I love him, but I also liked spending time with him. He was the best person that you could ever meet. However, I truly realized how deeply I loved him and how committed I was to him and our marriage when his health declined. Our marriage, from where we started to that point, had significantly changed as a result of the illness. Your test of love is when you still commit and love your spouse, even when you can no longer do the things you used to enjoy doing, when your body changes, and things don't function as they used to. Staying faithful and committed throughout it all is very important. Emotional intimacy becomes imperative, as you continue to pray for and love on your spouse.

You will develop inner-strength: I didn't know what my capacity was until I had to walk through caring for my husband during his illness. I saw my mother caring for my dad with ALS, for years. It made me uncomfortable, and I would think to myself, "How does she do it?" I thought to myself that I was not my mom, and I questioned my ability to do what she did, for years, for my dad. Somehow, God gave her the inner-strength and grace to care for my dad until his last breath. Somehow, the Lord gave me the same inner-strength to care for my husband,

and to do things I didn't think I would ever be comfortable doing. Something shifts when the one you love needs your help. You put aside pride and you do whatever you have to do in order to maintain the dignity of the one you love, and make sure they are receiving the best care that you can give them. It was during that time that I not only learned the depth of my love for my husband, but also the stuff I was made of that could handle whatever came our way.

You can grow in your faith in God: When what stands before you makes absolutely no sense, when doctors are giving you a negative prognosis, when you're tired and uncertain about what will happen, when you're feeling alone in your situation, the one thing you must do is lift your faith to Jesus Christ. It was my faith that allowed me to look at my husband's condition and still believe he was going to come out of it healed. I believed that our marriage would be stronger, and that we would tell this story one day and laugh about how God turned it around and worked it all out for our good. Faith in God is what keeps you sane.

WHEN TRAGEDY STRIKES

I n November 2018, my husband was getting excited about his favourite time of the year—Christmas. I don't know a person in this world that loves Christmastime the way my husband did. His eyes would light up at the sight of Christmas decorations. He was like a child in a candy store; it excited him to no end. This particular year, he wanted to put up the tree early in November. So I put it up for him, because the truth is, I personally don't get excited about Christmas; it's way too commercialized for me. My husband used to make fun and call me a Scrooge. Needless to say, I always decorated the house for him, because I knew how much it made him happy and how much he enjoyed it.

It had been a very stressful few months up until that point, and I really felt hopeful, as though things were turning in the right direction. I even remember telling my husband that things were turning around. We were getting things done that we had been putting off. I was happy. However, we still weren't seeing the improvements in Ian's health the way we would have liked, considering he had been on dialysis for a few months now. He continued to have shortness of breath, to feel lightheaded, to be tired all the time, and to have swelling in his legs.

A couple of weeks before Christmas, I was determined for us to get things done before we entered the new year. So in one week, we had a firm plan to tackle all our debt, get the car detailed, visit one of his younger brothers and his family who were going through a recent loss, and visit my mother and brother. I took him to his required specialist appointments, and it was determined that they would change the dialysis that he was using, because it was not helping. We even went to the lawyer's office to get our will drafted. I recall the conversation with the lawyer, and it will forever be in my memory. We went to him on a Friday, and he asked if Ian and I wanted to come to his home in Markham and sign off on the will on the Saturday. He told us a story of a client for whom he had drafted a will, but the client died the next day before signing. I thought to myself, "Ian is not going anywhere, so we can wait." I told the lawyer we would come on the Monday afternoon. I really didn't want to spend my Saturday at our lawyer's home, working on a will. So we confirmed for the Monday afternoon to sign our wills. After the meeting with our lawyer, we decided to go out for dinner and then watch a movie, one of our favourite things to do together.

The following day, I wasn't feeling great, and my husband went over to his parents' house, and most of his siblings, nieces, and nephews were also there. He brought food over and just enjoyed his time with them. Ian came back, as he normally would, experiencing shortness of breath. He walked in and leaned downward on the banister to catch his breath before going upstairs. He slowly made his way upstairs and sat on the bed. It looked like he was still trying to catch his breath, because he didn't speak right away. I asked Ian, "Do you want me to call the emergency?" He didn't respond. I asked him a second time, and this time he replied "No." His breathing eventually regulated, and he was okay. His shortness of breath was an ongoing issue that concerned me, because I didn't understand why he wasn't getting better.

Since the scare we had in the summer of almost losing Ian, I would wake up at times to check to ensure that he was still breathing. I was always happy that each morning he was breathing and still with us. We normally attended church together, but as his health declined, I attended more on my own. That particular Sunday was no different. I remember leaving the church that Sunday and someone asking how my husband was, and I remember saying, "Pray for him." After leaving, I did what I always do, I called Ian on the phone and talked with him on speaker phone as I drove. I asked him if there was anything he wanted me to pick up on my way back. That was something we always did; we were always in constant communication with each other, via text or phone call.

I arrived home, and Ian was there in our living room, just finishing up a meal. I gave him a bit of a hard time for waiting so late in the day to have his first meal. One of my husband's favourite places in our home was his office. He loved to go there for his quiet time—to meditate, watch videos, play games, work on business, or whatever he wanted. It was his spot in the house. While he was up in his office, I was participating in an online journaling session. My husband and I were supposed to go Christmas shopping for the nieces and nephews, but he texted me saying, "I'm so sorry, babe. I'm just so tired." After my class, Ian came downstairs willing to try to go shopping, but still feeling too tired, which was not uncommon. Since the decline of his health, he slept more than usual. I told him not to worry about it, and that we could shop for the kids another time. I had a couple of things on my list that I wanted to pick up at Walmart, and then I was going to grab us a couple of smoothies at our favourite spot.

I arrived in the parking lot at Walmart around 7:00 PM. I called my husband on the phone and shared with him that I had changed my mind about going to the smoothie spot we liked so much, because it was farther away, and I didn't want to spend too much time out of the house. I asked if he wanted an alternative to the smoothie, and he said no. I told him that I would pick up a few things at Walmart and then head back home. This particular Walmart was about five to ten minutes away from our house. On the phone, my husband sounded fine, and there was nothing alarming to cause me to be concerned. While I was shopping around in Walmart, our lawyer called me to answer some questions I had about the will, and, to be honest, that conversation delayed me, because I stopped what I was doing in Walmart to speak with the lawyer. By the time I walked through my house door, it was about 8:00 PM.

When I entered our home, there was a very loud noise coming from upstairs. My husband was listening to a preacher. I can't recall who it was that was preaching, but it was extremely loud, which was bizarre. I went upstairs, went to the washroom, and washed my hands. When I passed my husband's office to go to my washroom, he wasn't in his office chair. I assumed that he must have been in the washroom, and that whatever he was listening to was playing loudly on his computer. I entered his office to turn off the video, only to find Ian lying flat on his back, his eyes rolled back, and his tongue sticking out. I yelled out, "Oh my gosh, Ian!"

He was not moving, nor was he breathing, as I saw no movement of his chest. I dialed 9-1-1, this time trying to remain calm and not panic like I did the first time something like this happened. I was put on hold. I never knew it was possible to be put on hold for 9-1-1, when a person is having an emergency. I did my best to remain calm and wait patiently for a live person to come on the phone. Finally, a live person responded, and I explained that I had found my husband unconscious on the floor and that he was not breathing. The operator instructed me to start doing CPR, and I proceeded to do compressions, hoping that it would resuscitate Ian as we waited for the first responders to arrive. It didn't take long for the fire fighters, paramedics, and, later on, police to arrive. They went to work on my husband, and I immediately contacted Ian's parents' home. His younger brother answered, and I explained what was happening and shared that as the paramedics were doing their thing, I was going to pray.

It didn't take long for Ian's youngest brother, and his girlfriend at the time, to come and join me in praying for Ian. My mind was spinning. What was happening didn't feel real to me. In spite of all the craziness that was happening, I still never entertained death, not once. I believed, just like before, that Ian would regain consciousness. One of the officers came downstairs and told me that they were able to get a faint pulse, but they wanted to wait to make sure it was stronger before moving him down the stairs, since they would not be able to do CPR on the stairs. I said, "No problem." I was feeling optimistic. I knew Ian would bounce back. I got his stuff, and I was ready for them to bring him down, and I would ride with him in the ambulance. Unfortunately, that is not what happened. I still remember the paramedic that came to me as I stood in the kitchen. He said, "I am so, so sorry. Your husband is dead."

There must be a mistake, I thought to myself. At that point, nothing seemed real to me. I felt as if I was in a bad dream, and I just wanted to get up. *This could not be real. This man did not just tell me my husband was dead.* By then, family on both sides had arrived, and close family friends had gathered in the home. We were all in utter shock. Even though the paramedic had stated that there was nothing else they could do, that my husband was dead, we still weren't willing to give up. My current pastor arrived, because Ian's sister, who was a regular attendee of the church, had told him about the situation. He came and, eventually, after having to wait for the police to rule out foul play, he was allowed, along with my sister-in-law and youngest brother-in-law, to go into the room and pray. They prayed for nearly two hours for Ian to get up. I truly believed that he would. But God decided to take Ian home, as he did not get up. The pastor, my sister-in-law, and brother-in-law exited the room, because the caretakers for the funeral home had come for the body. I knelt at my husband's side, in utter shock and despair that he was actually gone. His spirit had left his body. Ian was very ill, and it was the complications of his diabetes, plus his kidney failure, that resulted in his death.

I watched as they carried my husband in a body bag and took him out of our home for the very last time. I stood outside for a moment. Some neighbours were outside wondering what had happened. I didn't have the words to speak to them. I thought about the number of times throughout the year that we had to have the ambulance come to the house, and the countless trips to the hospital. I could not have imagined that this was how our story would end.

It was devastating to have my husband die unexpectedly in our home. As if that was not enough, our will, the one that I said we could wait until Monday to sign, was not signed, and there we were on Sunday and the very thing I said wasn't going to happen did happen. Ian had died, and our will was not yet signed. Here began another saga of trials, pain, and frustration for me. I honestly didn't have time to process everything that I was feeling, because our affairs were not in order. I now had to coordinate his funeral, get the estate affairs in order, and try not to fall a part.

I called my lawyer and advised him of the situation. He proceeded to explain the process of probate to me, since I would need to go through that process, because there was no will. It would be a lengthy and costly process. I also contacted my dear friends and financial advisors who had already been working with us to cancel all of our debt. They were instrumental in guiding me every step of the way through the complete mess of our finances. At that moment in time, I saw no light at the end of the tunnel. I didn't know how I was going to get through this. That was the last blow. Up until then, I had stood strong, and I was encouraged and hopeful, believing that my husband was going to recover. And then he died.

I was experiencing a wide range of emotions. I kept feeling as if it was all a dream. Oddly enough, I was able to sleep in my own bed, and sleep with no problem. When I think back to that time, people were confused about my being able to sleep in my bed, and even to sleep at all. When I was sleeping, it was as if none of it was happening. In fact, it was the only time I had a break from the reality of what was now my life. I had to be very careful not to use sleep as a way to escape the world and to cope with my grief. I was very intentional about getting up and keeping active. I honestly didn't have a second to really rest, because there was always something for me to do. I had what felt like an endless list of to-dos. I remember my dear friend Shaun saying to me that I would not be able to truly grieve until it was all done. He encouraged me to stay strong and to keep going until everything was done.

During that time, I was grateful for the job I had worked at for ten years and that they had a good pension, since it was that pension that kept me afloat financially while we worked out my husband's work insurance. At that point, my husband and I had been married for ten years. August 2018 was our tenth year anniversary, and it would be the last one we celebrated together. My heart felt heavy every day. I spent my days on the phone, calling different service providers, notifying doctors and other pertinent parties of my husband's unexpected death. I remember sitting in the funeral home with my brother, father-in-law, and sister-in-law. I was there in body, but I wasn't there mentally. This entire thing seemed surreal. I wanted to press pause and just have things stop for a moment so I could catch my breath, but there was no stopping.

One of the traditions in the Caribbean church community is people coming to your house and gathering, as a way of comforting the family during the time of loss. In the past when my grandmother died, and then years later when my dad died, I didn't stick around for these visits, so I didn't know what they were like. I need you to understand the magnitude of what I was experiencing. The year prior, in January 2017, I had lost my father to ALS, so I was still grieving that loss with my mother and brother. Then in December 2018, just weeks before Christmas, my husband died. It felt like too much. I can honestly say that having people around me all the time was not helpful; I much preferred to be alone at times than to be in the crowds. People would gather, and we would have to make sure we had food to serve them. Every night for that first week, we were cleaning up after the guests and setting up to repeat the same thing, all over again, the next day. This routine became very draining for me, and not comforting at all. It was in moments like these that I would reach out to my cell phone and text Ian and crack jokes about the situation. Then I would realize, in that moment, that

I couldn't text him. I couldn't call him. He was gone. It was hard for me to be in those circles and try to be strong. Some days, I just had to walk away and go to my room and cry. Other days, I didn't make it to my room; I cried right there in front of the group of people that came. It was too much. It drained me more than it helped me. After one week of this type of gathering, I asked my father-in-law if we could move the visitations to their home, as I did not have the strength for them. He graciously agreed. My father-in-law was one of my greatest supporters during what was not only the loss of my husband but also the loss of his eldest son. We comforted each other through one of the darkest and hardest times of our lives.

One of the challenging things about losing someone is that people will say the stupidest things to you. I remember one person saying to me that maybe if I had been at home then help could have come for Ian sooner. I almost let that get into my head, but I had to shut it down very quickly. I knew in my heart that how Ian presented that night was no different than any other night. I could have been in the washroom, or at work on a night shift, and it could have happened. I quickly killed that negative seed that this person unknowingly was trying to plant. I rejected it before it took root.

I find that when you lose someone, people are uncomfortable around you; they don't quite know what to say. They may give you clichés or throw out a scripture verse, because, in their minds, it's fitting. Some try to make it better. The truth is, you can't make something like death better. I just have to go through it. Others made remarks about how young I am, and that I would marry again. What folks failed to realize was that I was not in search of another person; I only wanted my person. I was not interested in another man; I wanted my man. Something profound happened to me during that time: I strongly resolved that I would not marry again. That, by choice, this would be the end for me as a married woman. I have only wanted one husband, and I had one husband. So when we met with the funeral home, I made sure they understood that I wanted a plot that was deep enough to bury me also when the time came.

Why would God let me marry Ian knowing that he was going to die? I pondered this question. The truth is, I would not have become the person I am today had I not loved and shared a life with my husband, Ian. Though it has caused me so much pain to lose him, I am forever grateful for the years that we shared together. I'm better and stronger as a result of our life spent together. However, it didn't take away the pain and anger that I felt. I remember a moment when I was picking up patties to bring to my in-laws' house, for the guests that were coming to the home. As I stood in line for the order, I felt the rage bubbling up inside of me. I literally felt as if I was going to explode. Once my mom and I entered the car, I screamed at the top of my lungs, tears streaming down my face. I have never felt so powerless, so out of control, in my entire life. Everything was a mess, and there was nothing I could do about it. I couldn't fix it. It was all bigger than I was, and only Jesus Christ Himself could get me through this. The one person that I would share this burden with, and vent to, was gone. What was I supposed to do now? My best friend, the one I would bare my soul to, the one who, for twelve years, had loved me, accepted me, and stood by me through the good, bad, and ugly, was gone. There was such an emptiness inside of me. I was hollow. I can't even put the pain into words, because it's something I have never felt before. In one moment, Ian's death changed my life forever.

When someone dies, everyone gathers around, they call to check in, they attend the funeral, and then they naturally return to their lives. For me, there was no naturally returning to my life. Everything in my world had changed, and I couldn't stop it, nor could I control it. Ian has one sister born to his parents, and when I say his sister stood by me through this entire experience, she stood by me. She loved me like Johnathan and David in the Bible. For the first time, I let go and let someone else help me and care for me, as the weight of all that I was carrying was too much for me to bear alone. So she helped me tremendously through it, along with my mom and my father-in-law. In addition, my dear friends Shaun and Nicole guided me through all the financial pieces that, without their help, would have drowned me, and I would've likely lost everything. God sent me helpers.

One of the most common questions people asked me was, "How are you doing?" This is such a loaded question. Where do I even begin? If I say, "I'm okay," that understates the magnitude of stress that I was under. At the same time, I hadn't lost my mind, I was eating and sleeping, so all things considered, I was okay. It was always hard for me to answer this question, though, because what do you say? At the same time, it was strange for people to see me not losing my composure, not falling apart, still functional. I almost felt guilty for not presenting worse. The truth is, God would not allow me to fall apart. He wouldn't allow me to lose my mind and have this tragedy be the thing that buried me. This could have easily been the thing that broke me, but God would not allow it to happen. In fact, it was during this time that I realized why God had led me on that twenty-one-day fast. It was not for the reasons I had thought. God had other plans. I wanted desperately, when I went on that fast, to not be led by my emotions, but to be led by the Spirit of God. He led me on that fast to prepare me for Ian's death. I truly believe that the reason his passing did not break me into small little pieces was because God had prepared me in the spirit, without me even knowing. It is the only explanation for my strength. At times I questioned if I was really okay, or whether I was going to breakdown at some point. That moment never came. Yes, I would cry, but I never lost sight of the goodness of Jesus. I never hid away from the world. I never lost myself in depression. Rather, I clung closer to Jesus.

The other question people would ask was what they could do to help. That, too, was a very loaded question, because what came to my mind was, "Are you really ready for the answer to that question?" There were a lot of things people could have done for me that I didn't really feel comfortable asking for. As much as I had a strong support system around me, I still felt as though I was walking through the pain alone. There are just some experiences that others can't share in with you. Losing a husband is one of those things.

Ian died a couple weeks before Christmas. We, as a family, decided that we would still come together as Ian would have wanted us to. So we did. We gathered in the way that we traditionally would. We ate food, played games, and tried to enjoy each other, in spite of the very obvious person missing. I thank God for my nieces and nephews, because being around them brought me the greatest joy, and I couldn't cry in sorrow, because their happy faces brought me so much joy. We had a good Christmas, in spite of missing Ian. We missed his hearty laugh around the table as they played their games, and the infamous "PIT." He was such a bright light to the family. The big brother that all of the siblings loved, respected, and looked up to. He was loved by his parents, and pretty much anyone who met him.

I was dreading the end of the year, because I knew that what awaited me in the new year was the funeral. I remained in our matrimonial home the entire time. People didn't understand how I could be living in that big house all alone, but for some reason, I felt comfortable. It was still my home, and I shared great memories with my husband in that home. So I would sleep soundly every night. My sister would come and spend some nights with me, and she was a great support. My mom also came. Overall, I remained in the home until it was time for me to move out.

One of the other strange things that was bizarre to me during that process was the number of people that would reach out that weren't in regular relationship with me, but would offer to get together and then would never follow up and confirm a day and time. It was the strangest thing. I thought to myself, "Why even bother? Just give your condolences and don't even bother." I think it goes back to people not knowing what to say or how to act. They reach out and think perhaps offering to meet up for tea is the right thing to do, but think twice and just never reach out again to make it happen. Honestly, this happened on more than one occasion, and I got to the point where it didn't really bother me, as I had more things to concern myself with.

The other bizarre thing was folks who reached out, offering a shoulder to cry on and a listening ear, when they weren't actively in my life or my husband's life. That was a bit strange to me, as I'm not the type of person to reach out, in general, and even less so to someone that I'm not in close relationship with. It was a bit surprising to me that people would think that in a time like that I would want to bare my soul to them, when in the times when all was well there were no reach-outs or offers to connect. It wasn't for me, and I maintained a connection with those who were already there for me prior to my husband getting sick and dying, since that was my true tribe.

So we got to the day of the funeral. I made it through the viewing. I was blown away by the support that came from my husband's work colleagues, as well as my own. I had left that organization over a year ago and here my colleagues were coming out to support me. I was so incredibly moved by this gesture of kindness and love.

The funeral was a very difficult day for me. Probably one of the worst days of my life. I kept feeling as though I was having an out-of-body experience. *That could not be my husband lying in that coffin.* He laid there so peaceful, and all I wanted to say was, "GET UP, IAN!" I knew the spirit had left his physical body, but the whole thing seemed surreal. The funeral service was very hard for me. I sat there, tears streaming down my face, during the entire service. Before me were both a great picture of Ian smiling back at me and his coffin. I sat there as his wife, but I felt out of place, as if I didn't belong there. Some folks that came by clearly didn't know who I was, and asked if I was one of the sisters, and I had to clarify that I was his wife. I sat there and felt such a disconnect, as if, perhaps, I wasn't really Ian's wife, and maybe this was a dream and I really shouldn't be there. As if I never really existed in Ian's life, and it was a horrible mistake that I was there. I thought later that maybe if we had children then, perhaps, I wouldn't have felt so dismissed. Had it not been for Ian's god-brother who shared the eulogy and spoke about the date we got married, I would have forgotten that I had played such an important role in his life. For a moment, as I sat there, I almost got caught in my feelings, but there was no room for that, because I was consumed with so much grief and sorrow that I could not even dwell in that place for too long. I was thankful for the eulogy, because it helped me to confirm that what we shared was real, and that our marriage did matter. I had to focus on what was truth, and the truth was that Ian and I shared a remarkable relationship. I lived it, and so I found comfort in that and chose to let go of that day and put it behind me.

Funerals are very interesting, because people from all over will come to pay their respects, which I very much appreciated. The room was so full that I couldn't tell you who was there from who wasn't there. The thing I resent most about funerals is that people will come in numbers when someone dies, but when the person is alive, they are nowhere to be found. It matters not to the person who is dead that you have come to pay respects. What matters is what is done when the person is alive. When I think about the days, weeks, and months of Ian's declining health, feeling as though he didn't really have many friends; folks he thought were close friends weren't there, and it made him sad. If a handful of those that were at the funeral had given him a call, or had come to visit, that would have brought incredible joy to Ian when he was alive. So as I sat there feeling as if I didn't belong, amidst a room full of people paying their respects, I couldn't help but think, "Where was everyone all this time when he was alive?"

By God's grace, I made it through the funeral service, but then there was the grave. How I dreaded the grave. The finality of this man whom I had loved for twelve years, given my everything to, made sacrifices for, and taken care of, being put into the ground was too much. How? I could not comprehend what was happening. I put a final rose on his coffin, and as they were lowering his casket in the ground, I wailed. The sound that came out of me was a sound I had never heard before. It was such a deep sorrow. I thank God for my sister from the States, Taneya, that held me up as I wailed from the depths of my soul. A part of me died on that day. I lost something deep inside of me. There is an emptiness that was once filled by my husband. After he was laid to rest in the ground, we went to the reception hall. If it were up to me, I would have gone home to be alone, but I knew that would not be right, so I pushed myself to go. It was the last place I wanted to be.

You would have thought that at this point the worst was over, that now I could focus on grieving. The truth is, the worst was not over. My husband had died without signing our will, and so now I had to continue focusing on settling all the outstanding debts, putting our matrimonial home up for sale, and applying to probate court to become the executor of my husband's estate.

I learned some valuable lessons that will help others give better support to someone who has lost a special person in their life:

Avoid asking the question, "How can I help?": That question is loaded, and the person who has just lost someone has a billion things going on in their head. It's very difficult to narrow down how someone can help. Some actually want to help, while others say it because it seems like the right thing to say. The best way to help someone who has just lost someone is, firstly, to give a monetary gift. It cost anywhere between thirty to fifty thousand dollars to bury someone. So when in doubt of how to help, give a monetary gift. Secondly, bring food. It should never be the responsibility of the grieving family to have to host and provide food to the guests coming to support the family. Bring food to share amongst the guests, and help with the clean up at the end.

Avoid using clichés, or scriptural texts as clichés: Folks really want to try to make you feel better, so they will throw things out there in hopes that it will work. The truth is, it doesn't help. It's better for you to say, "I don't know what to say." That would be more appreciated. Even sitting in silence would be much better than making generic statements that aren't really comforting.

Do not put things on hold for another day: I put off signing our will. That decision was mine, and I own it. That costly mistake has forced me to stop procrastinating and putting things off. I don't put things off anymore, because I understand that nothing is guaranteed for tomorrow. I left my husband for one hour, and by the time I returned, he was dead. So I have learned not to leave anything to chance. If there is an issue, I'm going to address it in the moment. As far as I'm concerned, there is no tomorrow. All we have is today, this very moment.

Avoid asking the question, "How are you doing?" This is also a very loaded question. How can one possibly answer this question accurately? I get that people want to show that they care. What would be more appropriate is to say something like, "I'm thinking about you." Or "I'm praying for you." Offer to take the person out to dinner or tea. Offer to come over with some food, to watch some shows, or do some other activity. The truth is, someone who has lost a loved one is not doing fine. So instead of asking an impossible question for grieving people to answer, offer ways in which you can be a support to that person. Stop letting them work so hard to tell you what you can do. The person grieving is already going through a lot. It shouldn't be their job to try to make you feel better when they are the ones who have experienced the loss.

Avoid making stupid comments: It's important to be cognizant of the things you say to people who are grieving. Think before you speak. Ask yourself the question, "Would that be helpful to this person who is grieving?" If the answer is no, then don't say it. You will end up causing more harm than good. It defeats the entire purpose of what you were supposed to be accomplishing, which is providing comfort.

Avoid asking the grieving too many questions about what happened: No one wants to keep retelling and reliving the event, over and over, to satisfy your curiosity. It's painful. Give the grieving person some time. The story will come out soon enough. Asking twenty questions about how the person died is not helpful to the family member you are supposed to be comforting.

Grief will manifest differently for different people: How someone grieves may look different, and there should be no judgement. My father-in-law and I grieved very similarly. We had our moments when we would be in tears and hurting. At the same time, we had the ability to carry on conversations with people, and even laugh with people, in the midst of our pain. Just because we have the ability to do that doesn't mean we aren't hurting. We choose not to let the grief consume us. Some will see a person not falling apart and wonder if they even care that their loved one has died. Tread carefully. Just because it may not look like everyone else, doesn't mean the person is not hurting. Throughout this process, I have not looked like what I have been through, and that is because of the grace of Jesus Christ in my life.

Spend time now with those you love: Don't wait until a funeral to come with flowers and well wishes. Do that while the person is alive to enjoy it. The dead can't appreciate your appearance. They need it when they are alive. Be present, and make time for those you say you love.

Acknowledge the loss someone has experienced: I had some very bizarre experiences with people after my husband died. I would see people who knew my husband when he was alive and were aware of his death, and one of two things would happen: These folks would either make no mention of my husband being deceased, and interact with me as if nothing out of the ordinary happened, or they would act distant and cold around me as if I somehow offended them. Don't be in either of these scenarios. If you weren't at the funeral and didn't call, so be it. It's weird, and a lot worse for you to meet up with someone in the community or at an event and say nothing about the person's loss. You could at least say, "I was so sorry to hear of your loss." Saying nothing makes you look bad. Secondly, if you are that person who is giving the person who lost someone the cold shoulder, that also makes you look bad. Perhaps you are uncertain of how to interact, or of what to say. Keep it simple: "I was so sorry to hear of your loss." Nothing more is needed than that.

Avoid reaching out to someone who has experienced a recent loss to set up a date to go out, and then never follow up to actually do it: This was the thing that I found extremely weird. People reached out to me—folks that I wasn't really in close relationship with prior to my husband's death—saying things like, "We should go out for tea," or "We should get together." I would remain open and say, "Sure, let me know when and where." Then it would be crickets after that. Those individuals would never follow up with me or follow through with what they initially brought to my attention. Folks, it's better not to even extend an invitation, than to bring it up and then never follow through. It's not helpful, and it makes you look bad.

FAITH TRANSFORMATION

The night my husband died, I was in complete shock. The reality of what occurred seemed like a bad dream. It was hard to try to wrap my mind around the fact that my husband had died and would not be waking up again. However, I was not able to take the time to grieve, because I had another problem to address. The week leading up to my husband's death seemed like an amazing week. It was the most productive week for us. I felt so encouraged, as though things were about to turn around for us. In that week, it worked out that we met with family on both sides. After a long delay, we finally met with our lawyer to discuss our will and Power of Attorney. I recall, very clearly, sitting in the lawyer's office with my husband, going over our wishes and desires, should either of us die or both at the same time. I recall the lawyer sharing a story with us that he had a client that had met with him to discuss his will, and then the following day the client died before signing the will. Our lawyer offered to have Ian and I come to his house on the Saturday to sign the will. I remember saying to myself, "Ian is not going anywhere. We can wait until Monday." So I told the lawyer, "We will come back on Monday afternoon." I could never have anticipated what would happen next. Ian died that Sunday night, one day before we were scheduled to sign our will. So not only did I have to carry the weight of losing my husband unexpectedly and having to plan a funeral for him, but

I also had to deal with the fact that none of our affairs, including my husband's estate, was in order.

On the night that he died, while everyone was crying and still in shock, I had to wipe my tears and get into action to get things in order. I had to call my lawyer and learn what I needed to do for probate, because without a will, I would need to apply to the court in order to become the executor of my husband's estate. On the same night, I had to reach out to my financial advisors, as they had been helping us get all our debts settled, and we were just in the process of getting it all done before Ian died. I had to let them know the situation and proceed with the process of settling the debts as previously planned. This part of my journey was extremely difficult for me. I had no control over anything. I had to depend on third parties for everything within this process, which was the most uncomfortable and stretching thing for me. I remember my good friend and financial advisor saying to me, "Petra, you won't be able to grieve until this is all over." What stood before me seemed like an insurmountable mountain. Where would I find the strength to manage the pain I was feeling with this loss, and, at the same time, function daily to get things in order? Every day was exhausting. As I contacted various service providers to advise them of my husband's death, to start the process of applying for spousal support benefits, and to meet with the lawyers to start the probate process, I was told the process was long and could take anywhere between four months to a year.

In addition to all of that, I had to start thinking about selling my house. The mortgage was extremely high, more than I could manage by myself long-term. It was a house that was far too big for one person and a cat. So before I was even ready, I had to get the house ready to be listed for sale. That was a difficult process, and I was very thankful for the support from my family, along with Ian's family, who came to help sort through all his belongings and take what they wanted from his stuff. It was unreal to me how the death of one man had changed my entire life in one day. My future felt so uncertain. I honestly didn't know how long this process was going to take. I just kept on going. I kept getting up each morning, giving God thanks for another day, and kept doing what needed to be done.

In that season, I felt broken. One morning on my way to church, my sister-in-law Denise picked me up. I sat in the front seat, fighting back tears, as I passed many familiar places that Ian and I used to go together. I entered church that day feeling low. I couldn't even make it to my seat. I broke down in tears. I went to the back of the church to compose myself. I am very thankful for Supernatural Life Center, the pastors, and the church community. While I was in tears at the back of the church, the worship leader came alongside me and began to encourage me. I felt strengthened. I was able to wipe my tears, stand back up, and get myself ready for service.

It was incredible what God was doing in my life during those early months, shortly after the funeral. Every time I was in worship service at Supernatural Life Center, I would worship through many tears. God would consistently show me visions. On that day, when I was so broken and had to push my way through, God showed me a vision of Ian. It was vivid and felt incredibly real. I saw an imagine of my husband, and present with him was my late father and grandmother. In the vision, Ian reached down and touched my face, and he said to me, "It is well. It is well." I broke down in tears even more, as I needed to receive that comforting, to be reassured that it was well with his soul and that it is well with my soul. His death was so sudden and unexpected that it left me feeling hollow. It left me feeling angry, with a deep anguish.

The only escape I received from this reality was when I slept. When I slept, it was as if none of it had happened. Then I would wake up and realize it was all real. What was remarkable with God was that He continued to show me visions, and each vision illustrated my rising out of the ashes and experiencing breakthrough in my life. At no point did God leave me during this dark season.

I've always considered myself to be a strong person. I deal with situations as they come, and I've been able to get through difficult seasons in my life. This was different. This was unexpected, and it rocked me to the core. I had no blueprint or frame of reference. There was no one around me that could really relate to what I was feeling. Even though there were many around me who were grieving the loss of Ian, I had the double burden of not only grieving the loss of my husband, but also grieving the loss of what used to be my life. My identity had suddenly changed. My socio-economic status had changed. Everything that was seemingly a form of security for me had been taken away. I was faced with having to rebuild and start over, once everything was said and done. It was daunting, and I couldn't even wrap my mind around what life would look and feel like as a single woman, because I was still trying to wrap my mind around the fact that I would have to move from my matrimonial home. There was no time for me to adjust to this great loss. Things just kept changing in my world. Opposition just kept happening.

I remember reaching out to my pastor shortly after the funeral, and I spoke candidly about my need for help to walk through what I was facing. It was so much bigger than I. If it had not been for my pastors and the Supernatural Life Center, I don't know what would have happened to me. Coming to church was the only thing that made sense. It was a break from the chaos that had become my life. Every time I would go to service on the Tuesday and Wednesday night, as well as the Sunday service, day and night, there was always a message, either through Apostle Bible Davids or his wife, Prophetess Rebecca Bible-Davids, that spoke directly to what I was going through. Released within the message was the strategy of how to get through what I was experiencing, and the perspective that shifted my mindset.

As I continued to attend all the services weekly, God started to heal me and build up my boldness and strength. I'm a church baby, which means that when I was born, my parents were already born-again Christians, and they raised me in the church. I'm in my late thirties, and all this time I thought I had faith in God. The truth is, I didn't realize true faith in God until I had to walk through this incredible tragedy. I didn't truly understand what it meant to trust in God, until there were no other alternatives for me other than to trust in God and His plans for my life. Countless times during this journey I have felt tired and have felt that I didn't have anything left in me to keep going. Somehow, during my darkest and weakest moments, Jesus carried me and gave me the grace and the strength to keep on going.

People constantly speak of my resilience and strength. I can't take credit for this. I didn't have enough strength to deal with everything that followed my husband's death, never mind the death itself. I needed something bigger than myself, something supernatural, which could only come from God and God alone. What kept me pushing through the pain, confusion, anger, and emotional exhaustion was hope in Jesus Christ, and my belief that He created me for a purpose. I was still waking up every morning, so there was something still left for me to do on Earth that I hadn't accomplished yet. I kept fighting, because I desired to see what was on the other side of this loss and grief. There had to be a reason and purpose behind everything I was facing; otherwise, what was the point? I kept on pushing forward, believing that God had a greater plan for my life, and that this was not the end.

Attending church was my haven, the place I could let everything go. I could do the ugly cry, fall to my knees, and be free to reach out to God with no shame or embarrassment. It was the place I could escape from having to answer the question, "How are you doing?" It was a relief that not everyone at the church knew that I had just lost my husband, as I was still fairly new to the congregation. So I could focus on being ministered to, and I could focus on my own healing. Some would argue that I should have taken it easy, stayed home, given myself time to grieve and rest. My response was that I would have plenty of time to rest when I died. The fact that I was still alive meant that I was going to use my time to be in the house of God, where I found strength, clarity, and wisdom on how to navigate this difficult season.

Behind the scenes, I was dealing with having to justify who I was to my late husband, because we did not have a signed will. There was a level of humiliation and embarrassment. I understood that the banks had their protocols and procedures, but it didn't change the fact that I felt as if I wasn't Ian's wife. Almost as if I was a mistress or stray woman trying to scrap for what we had built together as husband and wife. It was hard. I hated having to go to the bank; it was a constant reminder of my hands being tied.

During this process, I learned that patience was an area that I needed development in. I like being in control. I'm a very task-oriented person. I'm decisive, and I like to get things done. In this process, it didn't matter that I would complete the applications that were required of me, as soon as I received them. It didn't matter that I would gather all the documentation requested in a timely manner. I still had to wait while others had control and decided when they would provide me with what I needed. For a type A personality like mine, waiting was the most challenging for me. The most frustrating. At the same time, it produced great faith, patience, and temperance within me. I just had to wait through the process. I had to stay on top of the service providers, because all I was to them was another number. It took months to work out the benefits and get those things settled and resolved.

The next challenge that required my faith was the process of selling my matrimonial home. Many people don't know that I remained in my home alone after my husband died. Of those who do know, some couldn't understand how I was able to do it. Even though my husband had died in the home, it was still the place where we shared wonderful memories, the place where we laughed, cried, and prayed together. So I felt at peace within my home. However, I was not willing to remain in that four-bedroom home, nor was I interested in renting it out. I knew I needed to move on.

The entire process felt surreal to me. As we packed away all of Ian's belongings, and sorted it amongst ourselves, it still felt unreal. I thank God for my mother and brother, who came one day to the house and helped me dispose of all the remaining solutions that Ian would use for his home dialysis. The thought of having to do it on my own was exhausting. I was thankful to my family for stepping in to help. I'm not one to ask for help. I'm usually the one to work it out on my own. However, in that season and that circumstance, I took the help where I could get it. I asked for the help that I needed.

Once all of Ian's personal items were distributed amongst family, and everything I was moving with was packed away, I staged the house, in hopes that it would sell quickly and I could bring closure to that chapter. Unfortunately, that was not the case. We had an amazing open house, based on the feedback from my real estate agent and mortgage broker. I even moved out of the house with my cat for three weeks to accommodate the process, so that buyers would visit an empty and staged house. I thought doing this would expedite the process. However, week after week went by, and there were no offers. People visited the house regularly but gave no offers. My cat was staying at the vet. There she was well taken care of, but she was experiencing significant anxiety to the point where she began to groom herself excessively and was losing her fur. Yet I continued to persist, in hopes that my house would sell. Then, to add insult to injury, a house on the same street as mine, with essentially the same things, was only on the market for one or two weeks and sold before mine. I recall that day so clearly. I was in my car, and I drove by this house with the huge SOLD sign on it. I drove around the corner and began to weep. I was tired. I just wanted it to be over. I couldn't even grieve properly, because there was always another form of resistance getting in my way that I had to address and deal with.

Not only were no offers coming in, but also when I would go to check on my house, strange things were happening. The people coming to look at my home had scratched some of the freshly painted kitchen cabinet doors. On another occasion, someone had pulled something out of the wall and left it there. On a different day, someone either spilt something on the toilet or had spit up something on it, and, instead of cleaning it up, just closed the door. At this point, I was so disgusted that people would come into my home and violate it that way. I had moved out of my home to make the process easier, but that was what I got for my efforts. I was hurt, frustrated, and uncertain of when this process would come to an end. My emotions went up and down. Again, I had to exercise patience, as there was really nothing else that I could do. My brokers spoke with the agents that had booked the viewing appointments, to inquire what the problem was. We finally learned that it was because I was not the executor of the estate. It was the uncertainty of not knowing when I would become the executor to legally be able to sell the house that had deterred people. My husband's name was the only name on the title, and, as a result, I had to wait to become the executor in order to sell it.

Finally, we received an offer, but the offer was so low that it was insulting. This real estate agent and her father were looking to take advantage of me, assuming I was desperate and would just give away my house to them. At the end of the day, we could not come to an agreement, so I walked. I decided at that point in time that I was simply going to trust the Lord. I didn't know how I would come through this situation, but I decided to believe God.

During this time, I started to investigate where I would live next. I realized the cost of living in the Greater Toronto Area was very high. Now I had to think as a single-income household and consider that I no longer had the financial partnership of my husband. I already knew that I didn't want to return to my full-time job, so in order to keep my expenses low, and not have to seek a full-time job, I started to look for a home outside of the community that I had lived in for most of my life. I went to a city that was about ninety minutes away. Now, it may seem insane that I would travel that far to live, and my family had their concerns about my being so far away. They worried that I might become depressed, not knowing anyone in that city. The truth is, as soon as I walked into the house, I knew it was my home. What was most appealing to me was the fact that the property was only a year old. The owners had taken great care of it and had done all the upgrades for me. Not to mention that it was a completely new community. I had no history attached there; I didn't have the weight that I carried within the community where I currently lived. Buying property within this new community was my little escape. I put in an offer, and it was accepted. It was our hope at that time that I would become executor in time to both sell my property in Brampton and close on my new property.

It would have been most ideal if things had worked out that way. Unfortunately, it did not work out that way. I had to contend with more challenges and more resistance. It had been four months, and I still had not received any word from the courthouse concerning the certificate of appointment as the executor of the estate. I decided that I would return home with my cat. If you are a cat lover, then you can understand how difficult it was for me to send my cat away and have her in boarding for forty days. When she returned home, she was experiencing so much anxiety that she had bald spots all over her body. I had to work at relaxing her for at least two weeks. I would play with her and pray over her, until she started to regain her confidence, and her fur returned. I stopped leaving my house to accommodate these agents and their clients, as those who had entered my home previously had failed to respect it, and I no longer trusted the process to allow people to be there without my presence. I stayed out of their way, but I was in the home.

Then something remarkable took place that I can't take any credit for, other than to say it was God's divine intervention. I had now had my house on the market for way too long, so we had to lower the price at this point. One, because of the length of time it was on the market, and, two, because the houses in my immediate area were selling for less, so we lowered it to a price that was comparable to what was being sold. By that point in the process, I had zero expectations. I decided to give it over to God. We were going through a month of fasting at my church, and the theme was "Stand Your Ground and Win." A couple and their real estate agent came to my home to view it. I stayed in my office on the main floor, out of their way. Prior to leaving, the real estate agent came to my office to let me know that they were leaving. She asked me if I was a woman of faith, as she sensed that I was. I confirmed that I was. I walked them to the door, and I felt as if they were people that I had met before, but I couldn't place them, nor could they place me in their memory. We stood there at my door for some time, chatting, laughing, and sharing, as though we were old friends. I parted ways with them, saying that whatever they decided to do, I wished them well, because purchasing a home was a big decision, and they were preparing to get married in the fall.

It turned out that the bride was a pastor, and they shared with me that they were having a conference, and she gave me the information to look them up on Facebook. When I looked her up on Facebook, I discovered how we knew each other. We were connected. On her page were pictures of two children for whom I was the adoption worker years ago. This pastor was the sister of the adopted father I had worked with to help finalize the adoption. We couldn't believe the coincidence and totally forgot that we had met on more than one occasion in the past. Prior to this couple realizing the connection, they had already decided that they wanted to buy my house. On top of that, they wanted to buy my house at the asking price, and all that I had to do was fix the roof and we had a deal. I was in awe of how God worked things out. It didn't make sense that for months I couldn't make any progress or get any offers. Then I realized the delay was because God was keeping the house for this couple. With all the love that Ian and I shared within that home, it needed to be sold to a couple that would cherish it and create new loving memories in it.

It felt as if I was experiencing another breakthrough, finally, after all the stress and negativity of trying to sell my house. Finally, I got a serious buyer, whom I absolutely loved. The only thing standing in my way now was that I was still not the executor of the estate. My buyers were okay with waiting, as they weren't looking to move in until after their marriage in the fall. I recalled my conversation with my estate lawyer prior to her going on vacation for a month. She shared with me that when you have a purchase and sales agreement, you can bring it to the court, and you can have it expedited. I was at the courthouse a week or so prior with a financial hardship letter, as it was costing me big time to continue to maintain the large mortgage and utility bills. I was depleting my savings to maintain this home, which was not good. Unfortunately, when I went to court the first time, they confirmed that there was nothing they could do, and that if I had a purchase and sales agreement, they could put it in the priority pile. So when I returned this time, I had a copy of my purchase and sales agreement. At this point, I had been waiting for six months. I advised them of the urgency of receiving this certificate of appointment to make me the executor of my husband's estate. I was told they were backlogged and that they originally had one person managing the files, and they had just added a second. I was told they would put my file in the priority section.

The pressure was on, and my back was against the wall. There was absolutely nothing I could do at this point. I had to wait for the court, which was slow like molasses. At the same time, the house that I put an offer on was closing, and I had not yet received the certificate that appointed me as executor. We were going into our last week of corporate fasting with my church, and the theme was "Stand Your Ground and Win." I prayed to God, and I told Him, "Whether you make a way for me in this situation or not, you are still God. I'm going to stand my ground and trust you to work everything out for my good." God surely showed up on my behalf, as I received word from my lawyer that I had officially been appointed as the executor of the estate, which meant I could both close on my deal with my Brampton home and close on my new property. If only it were that simple. I was delayed yet again. Because my lawyer's court processor had received previous instructions to pick up my certificate, when I went to the courthouse, I was told that it had already been taken. I had to wait an extra week for my lawyer to return from vacation so I could pick up my certificate. That meant I had to delay the closing on my new property and pay fees as a result of the delay.

Everywhere I turned during this period, I faced some type of challenge or resistance to receiving closure on this chapter. The remarkable thing was that, no matter what was thrown at me, I refused to back down. I kept on believing God. I kept going to church and serving. I continued to encourage others and lift my faith to God. Finally, I was able to close on my new home, and later close on my matrimonial home. Never had my faith been so tested in my entire life. I had just buried my husband on January 12, 2019, and instead of taking the time to grieve and heal, I had to keep it moving. There really was no choice in the matter. I had debts that needed to be settled, service providers that needed to be contacted, applications that needed to be filled out, and the list goes on. None of this made sense to me. I didn't question God as to why He allowed this to happen. I was more focused on getting through it. I kept showing up, because I refused to let the situation eat away at me and pull me into a dark hole that I couldn't get out of.

In my new home, I have a dry erase board that was left by the previous owners. On the board, I have written in BOLD letters, "THIS IS THE LORD'S HOUSE." Truly, God gave me this house. I need you to understand how supernatural the entire experience has been, and that I could not have done it without the Lord, and His gift of the incredible team at ShaCole Brokerage. I was able to buy my house while presenting very little income. My credit score was not the greatest, due to some bad choices over the years and debt. I had left my five-figures-a-month job a year prior to start an online business, and it had not yielded income to match what I was making at my full-time job. What I had at the time of this new mortgage application was a relief position at a women's shelter that provided me with casual hours. Plus a little over two hundred dollars a month that I received from Canada Pension Plan as a survivor benefit. That was all that was used to get a mortgage approved for me. God alone takes the credit for this. To this day, I stand in awe of how it happened. So for those who feel they will never get a house because of their credit, lack of income, or whatever the case may be, I want you to know that there are solutions available. God partnered me with the right brokerage, which advocated for me. The favour of God, and the help of this incredible team, made it possible for me to own my home by myself, with no co-signer.

In the space of six months, I had witnessed God cancel all my debts, which amounted to well over one-hundred-thousand dollars, sell my home to an incredible Christian couple, help me purchase a home with a mortgage that I could maintain without the need of a full-time job, and settle everything pertaining to my husband's estate. The day my husband died, everything felt dark, and I couldn't see the light on the other side. All I could do was take it one day at a time and face the challenges and hits as they came.

There were moments when I wondered if I was okay. I wondered if I was going to have a breakdown at some point. I kept waiting for the other shoe to drop, thinking that perhaps I was still in shock, and that it would just hit me all of a sudden. The moment never came. I had moments of tears, and screams of frustration and anger, along the way. However, I never withdrew into a dark hole. I was never angry at God, nor did I walk away from church. What this experience did was draw me much closer to Jesus than I have ever been. My faith grew, and I became stronger. My identity and purpose started to become even clearer. What I was doing in terms of business, prior to my husband's death, lost significance. I remember my pastor saying to me that I've been focusing on the minor, and now it was time to focus on the major. It was time to focus on what God had created me to do, so I could have a greater impact on the lives of others.

My entrepreneurial pursuits ceased from being solely about making money. It became more about fulfilling my purpose and my God-given assignment. I understood how frail and precious life was and that I could not, for one second, waste it on doing things that I had no interest or passion for. I couldn't be motivated by money, since it was not fulfilling enough to keep me doing it. I had to get in alignment with what God had put in my heart. So during the entire ordeal of trying to sell my home, I was working with a branding coach to craft my message and create a new brand that would reflect where I was now in my life. What was clear to me was that my brand was really my ministry, and I had to shift my focus to making my business Christ-centered. I could not have it any other way. I understood that I would lose followers, as prior to my husband's death I was known as "the Content Queen," adding value to various communities specific to social media marketing and content creation. However, after all that I had gone through with the loss of my husband, I felt a disconnect from doing that type of work in the marketplace.

God walked with me during this new season to not only help me navigate the loss of my husband, but to also help me rediscover my voice and purpose. In fact, He started to awaken some gifts that I had buried and forgotten about. Even though I had been sharing content on Facebook for four years, and what most would consider mini-blog posts, I had forgotten about my gift and passion for writing. God started to open my eyes to the gifts and passions that I already possessed. I didn't have to search to find new ones, because there were gifts and talents in me that needed to be activated.

God gave me the faith not to give up on the dream, and to continue to build the legacy that Ian and I started together.

We have no children, so I knew I had to stand in the gap and build and go far beyond what Ian and I had ever dreamed or imagined. Amid sorrow, God was turning my mourning into dancing. He gave me the greatest gift that one could possibly receive: He gave me hope. In 1 Corinthians 15:19 (KJV) the Bible says, *"If in this life only we have hope in Christ, we are of all men most miserable."* People wonder how it is possible that I can still smile and keep going. This Bible verse sums it up well. My hope in Christ is not limited to my life on this earth. I have hope in Christ for a life beyond this temporal world. I have hope that my husband, who was a devout Christian and man of God, is with Christ, and I will see him again in Heaven. If I didn't have that hope and revelation, I would have lost my way. There would be nothing left to keep me going. I would have given up already. What has kept me going strong is this revelation of Jesus Christ. 1 Thessalonians 4:16 (NLT) says, *"For the Lord himself will come down from heaven with a commanding shout, with the voice of the archangel, and with the trumpet call of God. First, the believers who have died will rise from their graves."* This life is not it. Understanding this revelation changed my perspective and how I looked at my situation. I couldn't be depressed, even though I missed my husband deeply. The reality of the Word of God was so powerful that it encouraged me.

I understood clearly that how I perceived my life and everything in it had to be in light of eternity. I couldn't just see things for what they were, or that would cause me to be depressed. I understood that everything in this life was temporal and had no real meaning or significance, outside of Jesus Christ. I realized that my focus had to be on Jesus Christ and completing the assignment He had for me before this world was even created. Ian was part of my story, but he was not the end of it. The very fact that God kept breathing air into my nostrils and waking me up was confirmation that He had an assignment for me. So instead of slowing down, or even stopping, I kept going.

It's important for you to understand that having this perspective does not negate the fact that I miss my husband daily. I still hurt over the loss, and it's likely that hurt will remain with me forever. What this revelation does is it gives me a perspective that allows this experience to become more bearable, and it gives me hope. I can channel my focus on helping others, while at the same time healing and growing stronger.

In the course of one year of dealing with all the firsts without my husband, while at the same time trying to clean up the estate and get my affairs in order, my faith went through a major transformation. I am grateful to my pastors, Apostle Bible Davids and Prophetess Rebecca Bible-Davids, because everything I have been going through since the death of my husband started to make sense. I started to understand, through the messages they would share at church, that the way to respond to adversity was through cultivating a spirit of faith. A supernatural faith that was not dependent on what I could see in the natural, but on the things I could see in the spiritual. During their sermons, I started to understand that I was going through challenges in order to build my capacity for where God was taking me in my next level. The biggest revelation that came clearly to me was that God was showing me that He was my source. Everything that could have been considered security for me had been stripped away—my husband, my full-time job, and my matrimonial home. God revealed to me that everything I needed would come through Him. I understood that I had to go through difficulties to show others that they can go through something traumatic, and faith in God cannot only get them through it but also get them through it stronger and better. Luke 12:15 (NLT) says, *"Beware! Guard against every kind of greed. Life is not measured by how much you own."* I learned that my worth was not measured by the things that I owned. In fact, things are irrelevant. Whenever I thought about money, I remembered my pastor saying in his message to the church, "I'm anointed to be resourced by the source." The source is Jesus Christ. I stopped chasing money and started to focus more on being in alignment with my purpose and Kingdom assignment. God helped me to be completely debt free, outside of my mortgage, for the first time in years. I realize that had I not submitted it all to Jesus Christ, I could have lost my mind. Folks have experienced less and have lost their way. God kept me, and because of that, I have rededicated my life to Jesus Christ and I'm on fire for God. There are no limits to what I will do for His Kingdom, to impact the lives of others.

Many have said, "Oh, you are young. You'll marry again." My response is, "No, I won't." Not because I can't, but more so because I have a call to singleness for the rest of my life. I strongly believe that I was only meant to have one husband. Shortly after Ian died, I already had the strong conviction that I would remain single for the rest of my life and serve the Lord. That doesn't make me sad. In fact, throughout this experience, I have received much peace. Philippians 4:7 (NLT) says, *"Then you will experience God's peace, which exceeds anything we can understand. His peace will guard your hearts and minds as you live in Christ Jesus."* This peace from God has me in awe, and is beyond my own understanding. As I continued on this journey, the peace of God only grew in my heart. The anger I had in the beginning started to subside and was replaced with love and gratitude. I can truly say the joy of the Lord has been my strength, and through it all, God has kept me. I will never be the same, again.

During this testing of faith, I learned some lessons that I hope can help encourage you as you face your testing:

Faith in God is not situational, it's a lifestyle: I had to learn that our faith is not limited to just getting us through a tough time, and then we return to being self-dependent. Faith is a lifestyle that we operate in every day of our lives. It's not simply during the bad times, but also in the good times that we must pray to God, in faith, for His leadership and direction.

You have more faith when you have less options: When I was in a situation where I had to depend on third parties to get me what I needed, I had no other options. I had no choice but to be patient and trust God to work in my favour. I find that when we have too many alternatives and options, we take matters into our own hands, and, ultimately, make the situation worse. When all we have is faith in God, we get out of the way and allow God to work on our behalf.

Your faith community matters: Having a strong support network within my family and church was essential to my healing and recovery. There was no way I would have made it out of that first year without strong leadership from my spiritual leaders and church community. Often, Satan, the enemy of our souls, will have us believe the lie that when we are going through something, we should stay secluded and separated. It's a lie from the pit of hell to have you remain at home, suffering in silence, believing that when you get your life back together and you are in a good place, that's when you should return to church. It's a lie. I learned that while I was broken, angry, hurt, and confused, that was the time I had to be in the house of God and stay connected to the altar and engaged in the Word of God that was being taught to me by my pastors. I could have stayed home and withdrawn from church, and no one would have blamed me. However, I would not have developed my faith and spiritual strength as I have, if I had isolated myself. I went to the best place, where God was speaking into my heart and giving me the tools I needed to get through every challenge that I was facing.

Seeing life in light of eternity brings perspective: As long as I saw my situation from the position of a victim and a place of self-pity, I would always be defeated, and there would have been no point pressing on. However, when I lived from the perspective that only what I do for Christ will last, I found hope and light in a very dark season. You begin to understand that there is more meaning to your life beyond material possessions. That everything that happens on Earth is temporal. That's why God encourages us in Matthew 6:33 (NLT) to *"Seek the Kingdom of God above all else, and live righteously, and he will give you everything you need."* It gives you perspective that God will take care of every need, no matter what it is. We must put our faith in Him.

Cultivate a heart of gratitude: As time went on in this journey, I moved from a place of hurt and anger to a place of love, peace, and gratitude. It was not easy to get to this place. However, I got there by surrendering how I was feeling to Jesus. I kept praying, fasting, and truly believing the Word of God and applying it to my life with the confidence that it was true. As I remained consistent, my heart would fill with peace whenever I thought about my husband. I was able to go to his gravesite and not cry. I was able to reflect on the fond memories and be thankful to God that I was given the opportunity to share in those wonderful moments. Living in a place of thankfulness created a peace that went beyond my understanding. My smile and joy were not forced; they were real because of what God was doing on the inside of me, through a posture of gratitude.

Understand that there is purpose in the pain: During this period, I started to read the book and daily devotional by T.D. Jakes titled *Crushing: God Turns Pressure into Power.* This was a timely book, because it gave me a greater perspective of how to perceive what I was going through. I began to understand that when we are being crushed, it's not God's way of punishing us or trying to break us. He is pruning us. He is taking us through the process that will allow us to produce fruit. It's the process that will draw the very best out of us and remove the very worst. If we allow ourselves to go through the process of crushing, we will develop a closer relationship and intimacy with God, ourselves, and other people. It's through the crushing process that you understand what stuff you are made of, and the capacity God has given to you to not only endure but to also overcome. Clarity and strength you never thought you had emerge during the crushing period. Without relationship with Jesus Christ, all that would be seen is the pain. Hope in Christ puts things into perspective and brings joy where there was once sorrow.

Surround yourself with people of faith: I can't stress enough how important this is. Just because someone says they are Christian doesn't mean they live a lifestyle of faith. You must protect and guard what you allow into your hearing and into your heart. I spent less time around people who were pessimistic. I spent less time around people who were always trying to point out to me why something could not work, or were too busy pointing out to me all the things that were wrong. I had to lovingly silence folks that were not speaking in faith, and instruct them that if they were going to speak to me, speak faith only. It's enough to be battling with your own mind, your own insecurities, and your own uncertainties. You don't need the help of others to feed into that. You need people around you who will speak life. I also understand that misery likes company, and some folks would rather wallow in misery than be lifted by words of faith. That was not me. I shut down every form of toxic and negative communication. That was what allowed me to keep my sanity. I would share my thoughts, hurts, and challenges with faith-filled people that I knew would pray and agree with me that all would be well.

BUILDING A LEGACY

I believe it's important to share my financial journey with you, so that you understand that, no matter where you might be financially, you are able to recover and turn things around.

As a child, I was not a person who liked to spend money; in fact, I was more of a saver. As I got older, that habit only continued. I was never a "girly girl," so spending money on clothes and material things was not a weakness for me. My weakness was actually food. Over the years, I would mainly spend my money on food and travel. One thing I was very intentional about as a young adult was to stay out of debt. I had excellent credit, to the point where when I purchased my first home with my husband, the broker working with us at the time was amazed at how high my credit score was. When I think back to the days of excellent credit, I wish I had received education around financial literacy. Perhaps that would have made all the difference and prevented me from engaging in some of the financial mistakes I made after getting married. Neither my husband nor I had the financial literacy to really make our money work for us. So even though we had a joint income of over six figures, we didn't understand what we really had. We were still thinking from the perspective that we needed more. I strongly believe that that's the problem for many working professionals. We have more than we realize. The problem is, we spend way more time consuming than we do producing.

Over time, I learned that having a good salary was not always a great thing, because we tend to use it as a security blanket to justify our bad spending habits. We know we have the cushion of a good job to help bail us out. Unconsciously, that was the behaviour that my husband and I displayed when it came to our money. We would spend money on travelling, eating out, buying gadgets, doing courses, and more. We purchased things that did not give us a return. So like anything, if you continue with this type of behaviour, it eventually catches up with you. Somehow we kept finding ourselves stuck in this ugly cycle. We would refinance, pay off the debt, vow to make changes, and then find ourselves in the same predicament, again, not understanding how we let it happen a second time. Once again, we refinanced our mortgage to pay off our debts, and then a third time we were back in debt. The cycle was vicious and very stressful.

During that time, we were not being faithful stewards of the money God had given us. We couldn't refinance again, or so we thought at the time. We had already done it twice. I had a line of credit that was maxed out, and I couldn't pay it off. At that point, we were living from paycheque to paycheque. I was doing what I know many people do: withdrawing the money from the line of credit and then putting the same money that you withdrew back in, so it looked like a payment. That was bad. I felt the stress of it hanging over us. I felt shame and embarrassment. It was 2015, and I couldn't go to our families about the situation, not because I felt they wouldn't help us, but more so because we made more money than our parents, and to be in so much debt that we had to ask for help was more than I could bear. I was trying hard to think of what else I could do to pay off our debt. The collections department was calling pretty regularly at that point, which was stressful. I thought about getting a second job, but the truth was that my full-time job at the time was already demanding, so I couldn't imagine mustering up the strength and energy to start a second job after finishing up at my first one.

The bank that held this line of credit became tired of sending me letters and receiving no response in terms of a resolution. So they took legal action in order to get their money back. I was so ignorant of these things. I had never had that type of experience before. I was scared of the unknown, and, besides my husband, I didn't know who else I could talk to. I remembered a lawyer that used to work at my company, and I asked him if he knew a lawyer that could help me. That was a big mistake, but it was out of my ignorance. I hired a lawyer that, in the long run, was taking my money but not really helping me. The experience stressed me out so much that I couldn't sleep or eat. It weighed on me every day. Then they set a pit bull paralegal on me that would call and basically harass me and try different ways to confuse and manipulate me to do what he and his clients wanted. Regardless of the fact that my lawyer advised that they not speak to me directly, he continued to persist.

The turnaround came when my husband and I went to meet with our friends out in Whitby. We were talking and enjoying each other's company. As he was sharing, he was describing helping people in situations like the one we were in. While we were there, I wanted to open up about what we were experiencing, but, again, I felt shame and embarrassment. When Ian and I left our friend's house, I talked it over with Ian and shared that I felt that we should share with our friend Shaun what we were going through and see how he can be of help. Ian agreed, and I ended up contacting Shaun. I explained our situation to him, and how

I totally forgot that that was his line of work; I could have saved myself a lot of money. I terminated my services with the lawyer I had hired and proceeded to work with Shaun.

It was during that experience that I learned the power of being a home owner and having an investment that you can leverage. I was enlightened to the fact that the money was in the house, and that what we needed to do was sell the house. We did not want the earnings from the house to go towards paying debts once again. I had to do what is called a Consumer Proposal. It's a softer way of saying bankruptcy, without being bankruptcy. It involves hiring a trustee company that is licensed to help you consolidate your debt and get rid of it. So I had to consolidate all my personal debts, close down all the credit cards, take a few sessions on financial literacy, and make monthly payments towards the debt consolidation. Then after a few months, I applied to a B-level credit company to start rebuilding my credit. When you file a consumer proposal, it remains on your credit history for three years after you have paid the balance in full.

We were able to successfully sell our first home and put about ten percent down on our second home, in my husband's name only. This should help you to understand why the estate situation I described earlier happened in the first place. Due to the consumer proposal, and my credit not being good, I could not be put on the title. My husband had the income and credit score to qualify for the house on his own. I cannot put into words how horrible not being on the title made me feel. How in the world did it get this bad? How did I manage to lose sight of the principles I had for years, as it pertained to debt and money, and find my credit pretty much ruined? I was grateful that Shaun and his wife, Nicole, were able to help us sell our home and purchase our new home. The plan had always been to put my name on the title, but, like many things in life, we put it off.

You would think that after everything we had just walked through that we would have never found ourselves in a financial bind ever again. Unfortunately, there we were, once again, back in debt, with credit cards nearly maxed out or completely maxed out. What was the problem? I think back to it now, and I don't understand how we kept falling into this situation. By fall 2016, my company went on strike, and that was a saving grace in a way, as that's what my husband had to communicate to debt collectors. Utility bills were either paid late or not paid at all. The main focus while I was on strike was to ensure that the mortgage was being paid. I can say that as bad as it may have seemed at the time, God still took care of us. We never lacked food, clothing, or shelter. Somehow, we were still able to travel on a cruise for my husband's fortieth birthday, plus host a birthday party with his close family and friends. We lacked nothing.

I returned to work in December 2016, after the strike was over, and that was the last straw for me. Then my dad died shortly afterwards in January 2017. When someone close to you dies, something shifts inside of you. You realize that you don't have time to waste doing things that no longer fulfill you. I was always complaining about my job at this point, and knew that emotionally and spiritually I felt depleted at that organization and could no longer continue there. In September 2017, I left to try to create an income through business, while my husband maintained his full-time job. Our debt situation still had not improved, but we were managing.

In 2018, I started to do some online projects that were generating some money, but not nearly enough to make a dent in our expenses. One of the things I am grateful for is working for an organization with a great pension. I had to take money from that pension to help cover the expenses. It was a tight financial season for us. We didn't have the excess cash or disposable income to fix our roof, which was due for replacement. Nor did we have the disposable income to buy a new dryer when ours stopped working. It was just the two of us, so I hang-dried our clothes. I suspect that there are many like us working professionals who go through situations like this in secrecy, due to shame and embarrassment. When you really think about it, what excuses did we have when we earned income that was more than the average household? I started to understand why banks didn't feel sorry for us, because they saw the amount of money we earned, and that we had good jobs. Money management is a huge issue for many. It's my hope that in sharing my story, the secrecy and shame can be removed, and this negative cycle can be broken.

We continued to receive calls from debt collectors, and by then, my husband's health had started to decline. So not only were we dealing with the financial pressures of debt collectors, but we were also dealing with my husband's declining health, which was impacting his ability to go to work and do his job. It was a stressful time, once again. I spoke very candidly to my husband as we celebrated our tenth year anniversary, and I vowed to him that this would be the last time we found ourselves in that situation. I spoke faith into him and our marriage. I shared with him that we had dwelt on that level long enough. That level was beneath us, and not what God had intended for us. Ian stood in agreement. I truly believed in my heart that we were at a turning point. I finally put down the pride and reached out to our friends Shaun and Nicole, once again. I was too embarrassed to go to them sooner, after everything they had done to help us the last time. However, I had to put pride aside and seek the help that I knew they could provide.

Shaun provided us with the different options that we could choose from. One of which was to sell our house and purchase outside of the Greater Toronto Area. That was not an idea we were fond of, because we didn't want to be far from family, not to mention my husband's kidneys were failing and he needed to attend multiple medical appointments in Brampton. The other suggestion was to purchase a home outside of the Greater Toronto Area and rent an apartment in Brampton. Again, that was not an idea we were fond of, because we didn't want to rent, nor did we want to live with our families, as we had become accustomed to our privacy. So the last option was to put a second mortgage on the house, and we would use the money to settle the outstanding debts we owed.

By November 2018, everything was coming together. We had filed our taxes and gotten some money back. We were also in negotiations with the banks to settle our debts so that we could pay significantly less than what was owed to them. I remember telling Ian how encouraged I felt. I was confident that we would come out of this situation. I had finished a twenty-one-day water fast in September, believing God for debt cancellation and healing in my husband's body. Things were moving in the right direction. Just when we were about to close everything off and finalize it all, Ian died unexpectedly. Can you imagine how I felt? That September I had started a new job as a casual relief worker at a women's shelter to help with some of the household expenses. However, I was prepared to return to a full-time job in the new year, and felt very optimistic that we would cancel all our debts and have a fresh start for good. We didn't get that chance, because God called Ian home.

So there I was, feeling grateful that we somehow made it thus far in what was undoubtedly a tough 2018. I was feeling optimistic that things were turning around, and then my husband died. It was like the wind was kicked out of me. *Now what? What do I do now?* The weight was too much for me to carry alone. I had to share with the family, on both sides, what we had been carrying on our own for some time now. I was grateful for the grace and compassion that was showed towards me, because the last thing I needed was a scolding. It was hard enough that Ian had died unexpectedly, now I had to clean up the mess on my own. Somehow, I found the grace and strength to jump through every hoop and do everything that was asked of me, in order to get through it on the other side.

It took a little over a year to clean up all the mess. I stand in awe of what I was able to accomplish with the help of ShaCole Brokerage. I remember Nicole saying to me that she doesn't know if she could have been as composed as I was through that season. Undoubtedly, that was one of the hardest, most challenging experiences of my entire life. I didn't know I had the capacity to endure something like that. I didn't know that I could come out of it better and stronger. However, by the grace of God, I did come out stronger. I spent eighty-five percent of 2019 cleaning up the mess, simply because we didn't plan. We didn't think that, as young as we were, something like that could ever happen to us. It was a costly mistake that has inspired me to be an advocate for change, to help families get their affairs in order and create a legacy and financial independence. The last thing anyone wants to be focusing on when they lose a loved one is finances.

In one year, I was able to cancel all of our debt combined, and now I am officially debt free. I'm rebuilding my credit, and my score is going up. I was able to sell my matrimonial home, purchase my own home outside of Toronto, without a co-signer and without a full-time job. In addition, I felt so moved by everything that I had been through that I felt a sense of urgency to be a solution to the problem and to help more families. I partnered with ShaCole Brokerage and completed my mortgage license. I'm currently working on getting my insurance agent license, as this is another area that people fail to consider when planning. I feel a sense of urgency to help raise awareness, so no other family has to go through what I experienced.

My experience with debt helped shape my character and build my faith even stronger. However, if I had to choose, I obviously would not have wanted to take that path. Once I officially became the executor of my husband's estate and I closed on both properties and secured all the investments, I immediately made arrangements with my estate lawyer to draft my will and powers of attorney. I have vowed to myself, and God, to never be a slave to the lender, again. I will never again find myself in such financial dependency that I need to rely on other systems and third parties. I am committed to creating financial independence and helping women, specifically, do the same. From now on, I will be a lender and not a borrower. My goal is to build wealth, through entrepreneurship, real estate, and investments.

I want to help people to avoid walking through this type of valley. I really hope you pay attention, take notes, and apply some of the lessons I learned during this season of my life.

Estate and succession planning are mandatory: It was irresponsible for my husband and I to not have put our affairs in order. We took for granted that life is short and things can happen beyond our control, and it left us unprepared. Succession and estate planning are less for those who have died and more so for the family members that are left behind. It's the family that is left behind that has to carry the weight of everything when it's not organized and in place. When things have been planned out in terms of life insurance policies, investments, and savings that are readily available when a loved one dies, there is no stress. It allows the family to focus solely on the grief of losing that loved one. I saw it happen when my dad died. They had all their affairs in order, and it was straightforward. Do it for your family; it's the responsible thing to do.

Check your work insurance policy: My husband and I didn't pay attention to what our benefits at work were concerning insurance. If you had asked me what my plan was, I would not have been able to tell you. So was the case with my husband. It was only when he died that I learned, and I had to go through a long process in order to access the funds necessary to assist with all the expenses. Make sure you not only know what type of plan you have, but also make sure you have updated your beneficiaries, which should include your current spouse and children.

Get insurance outside of your company: It's important to have a life insurance plan in case of death, and also understand that there are options as it pertains to insurance that can allow you to invest, save, and receive a return.

Always pay yourself: During my journey in the entrepreneurship world, the messaging around paying yourself has been consistent. You need to make building up your savings account a priority. The average home doesn't have an additional one thousand dollars in their bank account for emergencies, and that is a problem. What if your spouse falls sick and can no longer work, like mine did? What if your spouse were to die? When you look at your current bank accounts, do you have enough income that you could live on in order to survive? This is important. The truth is, my husband and I never took the time to really think about our financial future and plan it out. We took what we had for granted.

Acquire assets that you can leverage: This is one of the biggest lessons that I learned that I wish I had learned earlier in life. I didn't realize that the line of credits I had when my credit score was good could have been used to lend others money through a contractual agreement, where I would be the lender and someone else borrow money from me and pay me back with interest. I didn't realize, at the time, how I could have been leveraging my line of credit to make a down payment on a property to rent out. There are multiple ways to be creative and to leverage using money that is not your own money, so that you can get a return. Anything we spend money on that doesn't give us a return is a waste. If we are paying into something, there should be a way for us to be paid in return. Understand that your home is a huge asset. The equity in your home can be leveraged. I learned that when you have assets, you are able to make moves to turn your situation around. My first property was a condo, and had I known how to leverage it, I would have never sold it. I would have just rented it out, and would have still had that condo today, generating income and growing in equity.

Generate more than one stream of income: The issue for us was never really the debt, the issue was that we didn't have enough income in the end to cover all the expenses. Your salary is not enough to cover all the things that you are likely trying to do in your life. One stream of income can't finance the type of lifestyle that you desire. So in order to protect your time and give yourself more choices and control, having an additional income through a business is essential. It's no longer a luxury, it's a necessity.

Lower your expenses: This is a big one. Most people don't want to make lifestyle changes, and that's what keeps the cycle going. Adjustments have to be made. As a family, you have to decide what type of lifestyle you want, and what it will require to obtain that type of lifestyle. Something has to give, and you will have to make the decision on what that is, and stick to it. Dave Ramsey once said, "If you will live like no one else, later you can live like no one else." This saying is true, especially in the times when you are trying to cancel debt and turn your finances around.

Never cut back on your generosity: One of the reasons I believe my husband and I never lacked anything is that we were always generous—with our time and resources. We would always give in tithes and offering. Giving is powerful. Every time you sow a seed into the lives of others, God blesses you in return.

There is always a way out, no matter how bad it looks: Another great lesson I learned was that no matter how bad it may look, there is always a way out, and things can be turned around. The key that helped me turn my situation around as quickly as I did was that I was coachable, and I listened. Not only did I listen, but I also took action on what was recommended, based on expert advice from professionals who have helped others before me. I did everything my advisors told me to do, and that's why things turned around and worked in my favour. Can you imagine that with bad credit, a consumer proposal on my record, a casual relief job, and being a recent widow,

I was able to cancel all my debt and buy a house on my own? If this is not a testament of what can be accomplished, then I don't know what else will convince you. The key is that you have to be completely transparent about your situation, be coachable, listen, and take action. I'm a living, walking testimony that it can be done.

Draft a will and power of attorney for your health and property: Do not delay on this task. I think about the multiple times my husband and I would travel each year. If something had happened to us both, everything would have been a mess, and our families would have had to scramble to try to figure it all out. Be responsible. Think of your family that you would be leaving behind, and get that will and power of attorney done. Call and book an appointment with an estate lawyer today, if you haven't done so already. Funerals are costly, and so is probate. Avoid that entire ordeal, and get your affairs in order.

WHERE DO I GO FROM HERE?

Y ou would have thought that after the year I had—going through the funeral, all the challenges surrounding the sale of my house, and the long wait to be appointed the executor of my husband's estate—that I would feel great. However, the opposite occurred for me. After I finalized my own will and all my affairs were in order, I felt lost. For months, my days had been consumed with working out all the estate issues, settling debt, and moving. Now that it was over, I had to come to terms with the fact that I had to really start my new life as a single woman. I found myself crying more randomly; nothing specific would trigger it, the tears would just come. I started to question who I really was. I was uncertain about my identity and where I would go from here. I started to have moments of anxiety, thinking about life without my life partner. I didn't have that back up; it was just me. So much of who I have been and my identity was wrapped up in being Ian's wife. The person I was before becoming a wife was blurred. Now I had to rediscover that person and who I wanted to become.

The thought of creating a new life felt tiresome. I felt emotionally drained. Part of me just wanted to run, or at least press pause. Time just keeps going and it doesn't wait on you to figure things out. One thing that kept me pushing forward was the truth that God created me for a purpose. Before I ever met Ian,

God knew what He designed me to do. The fact that I was still alive meant that there was still work for me to do. I knew that if I continued to put my trust in Jesus Christ that He would give me the boldness and courage to create a new life.

One of the things that my best friend encouraged me to do was to journal, to start to track my journey and record my thoughts and feelings for the day. It has become one of the most therapeutic things I can do. I let out my frustrations, fears, triumphs, and the revelations and insights that God gives me on a daily and weekly basis. Journaling allows the free flow of expression. Instead of trying to articulate my thought to someone, I write it.

This stage of my life is quite interesting, because I'm learning how to walk a path in life that I have never walked before. The unknown can feel exciting and scary, all at the same time. One thing became perfectly clear: entrepreneurship was something that I would continue to pursue. I started to see how God moved me from a place of trying to chase quick money to a place of wanting to make a greater impact on the lives of others.

Over the last four years, I've been trying to focus my brand and decide on what I really want to be known for. I've had moments of uncertainty. I remember when my husband was alive, and I questioned whether I should keep the brand name Radical Change, thinking that perhaps people wouldn't get it. Ian told me to keep it, and encouraged me that being different was a good thing. In the summer, I tried to change my brand, but it never really took off for me. I wasn't connected to it in the same way. All my efforts to leave Radical Change had to do with my lack of confidence around it. However, it was clear to me that I connected with this brand name. It had my story, and when sharing it, I had more passion and conviction about it.

So I decided to return to what really resonated with me and the story I wanted to share to help women. In embracing it, God began to download more ideas and ways in which I could help other women with it.

At this stage of my journey, I had to learn to give myself grace and time to heal. This was also the time at which God started to reveal some deep-rooted hurts that I wasn't aware of. The truth is, these hurts had always been there, but I had buried them. It wasn't until all the estate stuff was finalized that now I had to work on myself. I had to confront the things that have been preventing me from growing to the next level, and the things that have kept me from wanting to open myself up to new relationships. This layer of truth and self-reflection was especially hard and uncomfortable, but very necessary. I started to take the time to understand myself more, and look deeper into my behaviour, feelings, and where they come from. As I dug deeper, I was able to see and understand more about myself, and I really began to heal in those areas.

There were many thoughts crossing my mind—the fact that I would be turning forty in a few months, that I would be travelling on my own, without my husband, for the first time, that I would be making life decisions without my life partner for the first time in ten years. For ten years, we consulted with each other on everything. Here I was now having to make decisions on my own. What became clear to me in my uncertainty was that I was not alone. Even though Ian was no longer with me, God had never left me.

I speak highly of my church community, specifically my pastors, Apostle Bible Davids and Prophetess Rebecca Bible-Davids, at Supernatural Life Center. It was not a mistake that they came to Toronto at the time that they did. Ian and I had only visited casually, and when Ian died their ministry was instrumental in my healing and in helping me to gain perspective during this journey. Every time I was in a broken and confused place, God would speak through my pastors the exact word that I needed to push me to my next level.

Apostle Bible Davids once preached a message that emphasized the fact that the challenges that we face in life are a part of a building process that is set up to increase our capacity for the assignment God has for us. I started to look at my circumstances differently. I started to understand that all that had occurred in my life in the last year was not meant to destroy me, but rather was intended to build my capacity for the assignment God has for me. I also realized that there were some things that God had to work out through me for me to be most effective in this next stage of my life. It was time for some cycles to end, and some bad habits to be replaced with better ones. Mindset shifts needed to take place. More love for myself and the person I was becoming was necessary for me to reach the next level, happier and freer.

Getting that understanding made me feel freer. Though this process of unmasking and confronting the things of my past that I had buried felt uncomfortable, God was giving me the grace to take the steps necessary to heal all of me, not just the parts of me that missed my husband, but also the hurt parts of me from my childhood that started to impact the type of adult I had become, and how I interacted with people. I gained some great insights into myself during this stage of my healing that I will share in hopes that it will help someone.

I learned some lessons in this part of my journey that I feel can help you as you go through your healing and self discovery:

Make time to understand who you are: We all live very busy lives. We are spouses, parents, professionals, friends, siblings, and the list goes on. We share pieces of ourselves with many different people. And it sometimes becomes easy to lose focus of a very important person. That person is you. In order to be the best version of yourself, you need to make time for yourself. You need to understand what makes you tick; what's behind the way you think, feel, and behave. I learned how important it is to understand your identity and not lose sight of it when you get married and have children. Staying in touch with who you intrinsically are as a person is huge and requires you to be intentional.

There is purpose in your pain: That's a hard pill to swallow, as I would have loved to have avoided going through the pain of losing my husband and everything that followed. However, had I not gone through these painful experiences, I would not have grown in my faith, character, and purpose. I've been reading the book *Crushing* by T.D. Jakes, which speaks specifically to what the crushing seasons of our life produces. Crushing always produces fruitfulness. It's in our mess that we discover our message, and our purpose is usually birthed during our seasons of extreme hardship and pain.

Do the work on yourself, no matter how uncomfortable: It's not usually fun when you have to be honest with yourself about some of the areas of yourself that aren't positive and that need work. It's hard to be honest about the feelings and thoughts that you walk around with that no one really knows exist—the negative self-talk, the self-doubt, the insecurities. I had to come face to face with all these things, because I felt God calling me to a higher level, and I knew I couldn't move forward until I let go of some of the baggage that was holding me down. It requires work, prayer, and a willingness to allow God to transform you. The ability to let go of people and the things folks have said and done to you over the years that have hurt you is easier said than done, but is necessary for your healing.

Change your perspective of your circumstances: Had I not gone through what I've just been through, this would be hard for me to say to someone. However, having lived through it, I know how important your perspective is to being able to come through extreme crushing seasons in your life. The wrong perspective will rob you of all your peace, and cause you to forget all the good that has occurred prior to the crushing. I had to learn gratitude in whatever circumstance I was facing. I had to learn how to see life through the eyes of God, in light of eternity, as opposed to what I see in the temporal here on Earth. Changing my perspective allowed me to stay focused on God and full of faith, instead of being depressed every day and unable to function. Your perspective will dictate how you show up each day.

Have faith in God as you walk an unknown path: Life would seem easier if we had a sense of what was happening next or knew exactly what things would look like. God doesn't give us the whole picture. He looks for our obedience to Him while we are going through a difficult time. It's because the path we are on is unknown to us that we ask God to order our steps, to guide us as we take steps towards our future and the destiny He has planned for us. Find comfort in the fact that your life is in the hands of God, and the outcome is guaranteed. Everything, no matter what you may be facing or have faced, is working out for your good. When we have that understanding of Christ in our lives, we win, regardless.

Do it scared: When major life challenges occur, or we are faced with having to take massive action in an area of our lives, it's normal to feel nervous. It's normal to feel a little apprehensive. Give yourself that grace, but don't stay there and let it paralyze you. Amid feeling uncertain and nervous, keep moving forward. It's in those moments when we stop relying on our own strength and start leaning on God as the source that He gives us the strength and the courage to do everything He has created and designed us to do. Don't let fear be the factor that keeps you from growing to your next level.

THE PEOPLE PLEASER

It took a complete year for me to settle all my household debt, and settle all the outstanding items related to my husband's estate. I was focused and driven, and I would not stop until it was all done. When it was all done, what I was left with was myself. What surfaced were the thoughts, feelings, and barriers that I carried long before I even met my husband. This was a time when God was confronting me with the stuff within myself that I needed to clean up before I could move to the next level that He was calling me to.

One of the well-kept secrets that many would be surprised to know is that for years I have battled with people pleasing. Looking at me and speaking with me, you would have never guessed that people pleasing was something that I struggled with. However, it has been something that I have battled in silence. It's a part of me that I have disliked, and I would be hard on myself about it, because I didn't want to feel or think this way. I didn't want to be easily hurt by people's rejection, indifference, or coldness towards me, and yet it would linger and have an impact on my life, particularly my thought life, in a very negative way.

For years, I have been very intentional about being kind, using humour, and trying to be inclusive and accepting of all people. I was often disappointed when that wasn't reciprocated. I somehow believed that because I was good to others, then they should like me and treat me well also. However, the opposite would happen. In fact, I have found, over the years, that people would treat me indifferently or unkindly without any reason. People would have an issue with my positivity. That one, until this day, confuses me. I guess misery likes company, and I was ruining that by seeking the positive outlook. Being impacted by negative feedback has been such an issue over the years that I could have thirty people giving me positive reinforcement, comments, and encouragement, and it would be that one negative response that would get me down. I would spend time questioning why that person was negative, and why they didn't like me. It sounds crazy as I write it, but it has been a reality for me for a long time. I would shrink inside and start to question my worth, because I was not successful in winning over everyone. The worth and the value I put on myself were misplaced. I was craving acceptance, even though I had a very loving family and wonderful friends. Still I felt as if I needed to have everyone on board. It has taken me years—and I'll be forty in a matter of days—to really understand the root of this problem and start to reprogram and condition my mind concerning it.

Losing my husband, and basically having to start my life over, has truly changed my life. I appreciate life more now, and I waste less time on things that are insignificant and have no bearing on my eternity with Christ, or on my purpose. I had to let go of people pleasing. One of the main things that God revealed to me about why I had to get over this issue was that it was the very thing that was keeping me delayed and preventing me from moving to the next level of my life. As long as I kept letting the opinions of other people dictate my thoughts and behaviour, I couldn't move forward with courage and power to do what He has designed me to do. God knew that for me to fulfill the assignment He had given me, I had to become unconcerned about the opinions of people, whether good or bad. I had to put my focus solely on the assignment He had given me, and He would be my source of strength and speak through me to make an impact.

I realized that I was giving away my power to people, and I was creating a more difficult time for myself. I believe that, more times than not, I created a negative narrative in my mind about people and circumstances that likely didn't even exist. We often misinterpret a person's facial expression, body language, or tone of voice. From that misinterpretation, a narrative is created. It becomes a story that we actually believe, and it impacts the way we treat those individuals, and how we feel and interact with them. I have been guilty of this. My perception was distorted for some time, and I underwent needless pain.

I can't say that it's something that is totally gone, but my self-awareness has increased. I'm more intentional. I don't let negative narratives fester; I deal with them right away and replace them with what is true. What has helped me tremendously is prayer, reading the Word of God, and surrounding myself with positive people who actually see me for who I really am. Never again will I let people who know me, or don't know me, define who I am. God has done that, and it's from Him that I draw my strength.

One of the biggest "Aha" moments for me came in examining the life of Jesus and His ministry on Earth. I'm a church baby, who grew up in church. However, ever since my husband died, I've been seeing the Scriptures differently. I'm gaining insight and revelation that I didn't necessarily have before. For me, the Word of God is not a fairy tale. I believe it is the truth and the ultimate authority in my life. It has been the very thing to heal me and transform me during my season of loss. In December 2019, I spent twenty-four days reading a chapter a day in the Book of Luke, leading up to Christmas Day. I got the idea off of Facebook. It helped me to appreciate Christmas much more. However, it did something even greater. I was able to learn from Jesus's life, and learn how to apply those lessons to my own life. Jesus is the Son of God. He came from God, and He was given a message to give to the world. His assignment was to preach the Kingdom of God, and to die for the sins of the world. That was no easy assignment.

Jesus knew who He was, and was confident in the fact that His Father had sent Him. However, there were many religious leaders who questioned His authority and identity, even when Jesus was doing good on Earth—He was sharing a message of hope and salvation; He was healing all sicknesses and healing people of evil spirits; He was light on Earth. In spite of all that good, Jesus still endured significant criticism and hatred. These religious leaders sought ways to kill Him. They looked for ways to accuse Him, to trick Him into saying something that would give them further cause to bring Him down. They tried to discourage Him from fulfilling His purpose. There were threats, mockery, lies, and the list goes on. What hit me like a ton of bricks in reading about Jesus Christ and His life on Earth was that He never once allowed any of this negativity to deter Him from His purpose. He didn't allow their lack of belief in who He was to change His confidence and assurance of His own identity and assignment. Jesus consistently shared about the Father, being sent by Him, and His message to the world. Jesus did not back down, nor did He dim His light to satisfy the critics. He had a clear purpose, and He showed up, whether folks liked Him or not. He showed up, whether folks received His message or not. He stayed focused. And in order to keep His focus under such resistance and opposition, He remained consistent in His private prayer life. It reminds me of a sermon my husband once gave titled "More Prayer, More Power."

This was not the first time that I learned about Jesus's ministry on Earth and what He endured. However, this time it impacted me differently. I saw His example in relation to myself. I saw that God had given me an assignment, and I have allowed the opinions and indifference of others to deter me, to cause me to shrink back and dim my light. It was in that moment that I realized I could never be that people-pleasing person anymore. I am accountable to Jesus Christ for what I do and don't do. So my perspective and my focus have shifted. The assignment God has given us is not about us. Rarely is it comfortable, particularly when you go against the grain and do what people don't expect.

Growing up, I loved to wear pants, because I was most comfortable in them. However, around grade six my mom told me I could no longer wear pants out in public. The church community I grew up in didn't believe in women wearing pants. For a long time, I dressed in a way that would satisfy my parents and the church community that I belonged to at the time. I also always wanted to dye my hair red. However, again, I knew that this was not what people expected of me. I got tired of doing what everyone expected. It didn't serve me, and definitely didn't help others. The same year I lost my father to ALS, I went to a professional hair stylist and coloured my full head bright, fiery red. I had the support of my loving husband. Sure, folks were surprised, but it was the beginning of something very powerful for me—freedom. Freedom from the opinions and criticisms of other people.

In this season of my life, I've been learning to not be afraid of letting go and being bold, fierce, passionate, and outgoing. I restricted myself for a long time, concerned that I was too loud, too outgoing, and too much for people. I've come to understand that those who don't like my personality are simply not my people, and that's okay. I don't have to keep trying to change myself to fit into the mold others have for me. It's exhausting and, quite frankly, impossible. People are fickle and change like the wind. Moving forward, as I start chapter forty of my life, my goal is to please God, be myself, and love who God has created me to be. I feel free, and I'm excited to continue to grow.

I've learned a few things from my people-pleasing journey that I believe will be helpful to you:

It's impossible to please everyone: Time and energy are wasted trying to please everyone. Let the driving force for what we do be centred on our purpose and what God has created us to do. Let it be focused on being of service to others in a way that will help them and bring about change.

Detach yourself from negativity and toxic people: I had to make a conscious decision to limit my time with negative people, even if they were friends or family. Family and friends may love you, but unintentionally give off negative energy that takes away from you instead of add to your life. Spend more time in places where you are celebrated rather than tolerated. Pay attention to the shows you watch, and the things you listen to and allow into your life. Surround yourself with the words, images, and people that ignite you and empower you to live your best life

Hurt people hurt people. It has nothing to do with you: My background is social work, and I've come to understand, over the years, that people are hurting. More times than not, their issue with you has nothing to do with you. Sometimes something about you triggers in them something from their past. Other times, it's simply the old case of jealousy. I've learned that, oftentimes, you aren't the problem, the other person is. It's our responsibility to not allow their problem to become our problem. That knowledge alone has freed me a lot. When someone comes to me with a negative attitude or indifference, I check my mindset and keep it moving. It has nothing to do with me. Refuse to give people the power to control and impact your emotions, thoughts, and behaviours.

People pleasing will not bring you happiness: Trying to please everyone is misery. You end up being hurt often. If someone has decided to feel a certain way about you, it won't matter what you do. Even if they do give you attention, it still won't make you happy. I've learned to accept and embrace who I am, and love the person God has created me to be. Cultivate the peace of God. Be okay with everyone not wanting to connect or be your friend. This is a big world with incredible people who would love nothing more than to be a part of your tribe. Focus on serving and connecting with those people. Don't hang around people that don't appreciate you and see you for the gem that you are.

Life is too short to limit yourself to the opinions of others: One of the greatest lessons I learned from my husband and his death is that life is short. It's too short to carry unnecessary baggage and pain. Make a commitment to yourself to let go of all that negative baggage. It doesn't happen overnight. It's a commitment to consistently renew your mind daily. I renew my mind with the Word of God. It may be different for you. I approach life with a sense of urgency. I don't have time to be concerned with the haters, because there is an assignment from

God given to me that I must accomplish before it's my time to be with Him in Heaven. Shut down anything that distracts you from your purpose alignment.

Embrace the person you are, and the person you are becoming: Before you can accept the love of others, you have to be able to love and accept yourself. When you do this, what radiates from you is love and light. Don't waste one more day trying to get attention and love from others. Love yourself, and love others as God has instructed us to do. In doing so, you will show up in life powerful and *free*.

PUTTING BACK THE BROKEN PIECES

R arely do we just have behaviours, thoughts, and attitudes that did not originate from some place. During my season of recovery and healing, I had to connect with where my pain and distorted truth came from. What was the root of my becoming a people pleaser in the first place? I took the time to do this exercise, and let me tell you, it was not easy. It opened old wounds that were never really healed or dealt with. Over the years, I learned how to just push through and keep going, and not really deal with those things that were hurtful and painful. As God was dealing with me, He was showing me that I could not enter a new decade and step into the assignment He has called me to while still carrying the weight and hurts of the past. He knew that as He elevated me in my purpose, I could not continue to care so much about the opinions of others; I wouldn't last a day. So He helped me to deal with, and work through, it.

Understanding the root helped me to realize that I had developed walls, mostly for survival. I didn't realize that I had done this, until my husband died and I realized that I had built walls around my heart to keep me from being hurt by people who didn't mean me well. However, I've learned that in keeping walls up to protect myself from those who have ill intent, I also keep out those who truly care and want to express their love towards me. It has been hard for me to accept the love, compliments, and accolades over the years. I've had to grow in this area, over time. It all traces back to my experiences growing up as a child in church. I've heard people talk about "church hurt," and have often used that as their reason for walking away from their relationship with Jesus, or turning their back on the church. Though I have experienced some of my most hurtful experiences within the church, I never once entertained the idea of walking away from my relationship with Jesus or the church. I recently listened to a conversation regarding this issue, and it was stated so eloquently: It's not the institution of the church that causes the pain, it comes down to specific individuals that cause specific pain. Therefore, some reframing needs to take place when we describe hurt. We should not attach it to the institution of the church, but to specific people and situations.

I remember a specific incident. I was eight or nine years old. At that time, I was still very sensitive in liking everyone and wanting everyone to like me, too. I was sensitive, in that my feelings would get easily hurt, and I would cry. I remember a couple of girls making fun of me about something, I can't even recall what it was that they were referring to. However, I do recall one of them looking at me as my eyes began to well up with water, and she said, "What? Are you going to cry now?" I remember her motioning like a cry baby. Tears began to roll down my face. It was in that moment that my wall got built. I had determined in my heart that I would not let people see how they were getting to me. I would not let them have the satisfaction of seeing me cry. I would not let people hurt me in that way. That was the moment my wall went up, and it impacted my life and relationships for years afterwards. That one moment in time, seeming so simple amongst children, hurt me deeply.

After that, I carried a tough exterior. I wouldn't share my heart as easily. And it only got worse when I would take a chance and let my guard down and share my feelings and thoughts with someone, only to have everything I shared in secret be disclosed to others. I would build my walls even more. I resolved that I couldn't trust people. Sadly, it was mainly folks in the church that I had this issue with. So I didn't let folks in church get close to me. I would keep conversations surface level, because, in the back of my mind, I was always concerned about how things could be used against me to bring me down.

You would have never thought I battled with this growing up in church, as I would be called on to speak in my church regularly. Hearing me, you would believe I was the fiercest, most fearless person in the room. That's the way God would use me. What folks didn't know was that there was a constant battle that I fought—never feeling like I fit in, always questioning the motives of others, not knowing who I could really trust and let my guard down with, having folks tell me to my face that they've hated me for a long time and have not known why. I went through being lied on, talked about, called "stuck up," you name it. I didn't let people get to know me, because there was no trust. In not knowing me or understanding me, it became easy for people to come to their own conclusions and misread my demeanor. The pressure was also on to be at my best, because my parents and grandmother were leaders within the church. So it was a lonely place for me.

The good thing I can say is that it caused me to grow in my prayer life. Worship, praise, prayer, and reading the Bible were what kept me sane. They got me through many storms of heartache and pain. I would preach with a heavy heart, and God would continue to use me. As He used me, I would find ways to shrink back. Being different in this way was not a likeable feature. Sometimes I wondered if I were ordinary, then maybe I would have less opposition. I tried to dim my light and shrink back so others could have the spotlight. I never sought the spotlight, but it seemed to find me. It didn't make it easier when folks would compare others to me, and pass remarks like, "Why don't you be more like Sis. Petra?" It was the most uncomfortable experience.

I remember one time being asked to lead a song, and one of the adults saying that I was always "hogging the mic." I never wanted the mic, and hearing that remark made me want to avoid it even more. No such luck, as I could not suppress what God had put inside of me. I would try to be quieter, less loud, less fiery, but it would just bubble inside of me and explode. This is who God designed me to be. I was trying to suppress who I was because I wanted to be normal. I wanted to be accepted and liked. It was hard. I thrived in school, and never experienced the level of loneliness in school that I did within the church. That being said, I had my own relationship with Jesus Christ that could not be affected by how others treated me. So I kept going to church, and kept serving, because I genuinely loved people and wanted to see others grow and win. However, what resulted was the wall that I put up. I realize now that those who said and did things that hurt me deep down didn't realize the impact of their actions and the harm that they were causing. I have also come to understand that the enemy of my soul, Satan, has been trying to silence me from the day I accepted Jesus into my heart at the age of eight years old. He knew that if I discovered how much God loved me, and what He had called me to do, millions of people would be blessed, healed, and delivered. So he has worked hard to shut me up. The thing is that no matter how dark my valleys got, I could not stop being who God created me to be. My calling would manifest itself in school presentations, in group projects, in writing assignments. My purpose and gifts have always been evident, even when I tried to push them down or brush them off.

I understand now why I brushed them off and ran from the call of God on my life. I didn't want to give people more reasons to dislike me. I didn't want to stand out more than I already did. So I downplayed my abilities. It was the people pleasing thing, and it didn't change anything. I continued to feel bad. I would pray hard, preach hard, sing hard, and that was how I got through those challenging times of my life. In spite of how people treated me, I would always be respectful and kind. Wherever I went, there would always be a woman, oddly enough, that, for whatever reason, would have an attitude towards me. I never quite understood it. I was very intentional about being kind, but, for whatever reason, there would be another woman sizing me up, giving me the cold shoulder, and being very unwelcoming.

It always confused me when people said, "I love you," but their actions communicated something totally opposite. It has always left me puzzled. I allowed this duplicity to consume my thoughts and cause me unnecessary heartache and pain for years. As I got older, I started to confront my need for acceptance, because it was causing me needless distress. I shared these secret thoughts and feelings with the one I trusted most in the world—my husband. I felt so secure in his love and friendship that I accepted the fact that I wouldn't have many meaningful relationships with women, especially Christian women, which sounds sad, but that was my experience.

When my husband died, I came face to face with the truth that he was my security blanket. I didn't have to put myself out there, nor did I put much effort into cultivating new relationships with other women. Then he died, and I found myself realizing that I have kept this wall of protection to my own detriment. In order to grow, I had to take the leap and let people in. I had to slowly take down the wall that had been put up for years, and let God lead the right people into my life. My husband's death made me realize the importance of broadening my circle and cultivating real relationships with women, including Christian women. As scary as it may feel, and as uncomfortable as it may be, I realized that this was a step that I had to take. So I started to connect with new women, and enter new spaces. I've been giving myself the grace to heal in this area. In doing so, I've already started to attract incredible women into my life that I believe are sent by God, who has been positioning me in the right place with the right people.

One of the things God began to minister to me about is creating a community for women to start having these transparent conversations. I felt this need during a time when I was frustrated over yet another woman who was acting negatively, caught up in her feelings, which impacted how she interacted with me. I was communicating my frustration to God about the entire thing. It was then that He started to speak to me about looking for spaces that could facilitate the type of interpersonal and genuine connectedness that I expressed to others. I heard His still, small voice say, "Stop looking for it, and start creating it." So I reluctantly said, "Yes," and I have committed to being the change I want to see.

I learned a few things from this experience that I believe can help you:

Do not leave hurt unaddressed: I was young and likely should have reached out to talk to someone about my hurt long before I did, so that it would not have continued to be an issue in my adult life. I've learned the importance of connecting with someone you can trust, and releasing the hurt. Sometimes that may mean speaking to someone professionally.

Never close yourself off to love and healthy relationships out of fear: I get that it's a risk, and that loving people results in hurt sometimes, whether intentional or unintentional. That being said, God made us to be social beings. We need genuine connections with other people. Keeping walls up causes us to miss out on the wonderful people that we could meet and have relationships with.

Build your own tribe: I've learned the importance of connecting with people whom you desire to be a part of your tribe. Individuals who have similar values, and who are genuine. People who will add value to your life, and who will have a reciprocal exchange with you, instead of you always giving. You need a circle of friends that can fill up your tank, as you pour out to others.

Don't dim your light to make others feel better about themselves: Never dim your light, thinking that it will make someone else feel better about themselves. The personal dissatisfaction someone has about themselves has nothing to do with you. Your shrinking back does not help them shine. There is a greater issue going on within that other person that they must work through, with help. Don't stop being a bright light. Shine bright, with no apology. Understand that when you shine bright, you are being a blessing to others.

Work on developing yourself every single day: We have to work on ourselves long before we start to criticize other people. Do a self-examination. What are some areas that could use improvement? What can you do differently today in the form of an action step so that you can grow and improve in those areas? Show up as your best self, always.

CHANGE THE DEFAULT SETTING

One of the things I've battled with over the years is my thought life. The agonizing battle within the mind. What I discovered by the end of settling my late husband's estate was that I had developed a conditioned response that I refer to as the "Default Setting." My mind would automatically go to a negative narrative as it pertains to other people and their behaviour towards me. I would automatically think the worst case scenario. It was painful to live this way. The narrative that I formed in my mind became so real that it would impact how I felt about and interacted with specific people. I would avoid those individuals. In my mind, they didn't like me and didn't want me around. So just hearing their name, seeing their picture, or seeing them at the same event would cause a reaction in me. I didn't show it, but I would be uncomfortable around those individuals. In my mind, I carried this faulty narrative.

Looking at me and seeing how I engage with people, you would never think that I carried this inner battle and struggle. I'm naturally social, friendly, and outgoing. Yet in spite of having that type of personality, I had this hidden battle that I would fight. Over the years, it would drain me emotionally. These thoughts and feelings would steal my joy, every time. They left me feeling inadequate, intimidated, small, and insignificant.

I used to wonder if those people could see or feel my discomfort and the awkwardness in our interaction. There is a distinct difference that takes place within me whenever I'm very comfortable with a person, as opposed to when I'm not. I hated feeling discomfort. I remember thinking to myself as a child that when I become an adult, I don't want to feel this way. I don't want to have these negative thoughts about myself and the way I believe some people perceive me. I believe a lot of times relationships with those individuals didn't improve because I allowed my narrative about them to remain the same. So my behaviour and attitude towards them didn't change. Deep down I knew this was hindering me from growing. I knew that these thoughts needed to be reframed in a way that actually reflected what was true. It's incredible how we can misinterpret a person's body language, words, and behaviour. Having a simple conversation could often clear up a lot of misunderstandings. However, I didn't always have the courage to have these courageous conversations. That courage only developed for me later on in life.

I got to a point where I was tired of giving away my joy. I was tired of allowing my mind to just move randomly to any thought that formed. I let thoughts come in, and I left them unchallenged, which was debilitating. At times I felt like an imposter, which is huge for me, because I pride myself on being transparent and authentic. However, in those instances, I would be smiling on the outside, but inside I would be feeling uncomfortable. I had the walls up to protect myself from further heartbreak, and I had the battle in my mind about what I perceived people felt or thought about me.

Things started to shift for me in this area of my life in 2017, when I resigned from my full-time job of ten years. I was getting to a place where I couldn't base my decisions on what other people said or how they felt. I also couldn't base my decisions on whether people affirmed or validated me in what I was doing. All I knew moving forward was that I needed to radically change my life, and I needed to grow. No one else was going to do this work for me; I had to do it for myself.

I started to do the work on myself. When my husband died, I believe that was the pinnacle of my self-awareness to the things about myself that I didn't like and that needed to change in order for me to have a greater impact in the area of my calling. To continue operating with this negative narrative was disempowering, and it limited my ability to form new, healthy relationships, and to evolve and grow in my next level of life. So as uncomfortable as it was to look myself in the mirror and address the issues that have been a heavy weight in my life, I did it. I did it mainly because I know that it is the will of Jesus Christ for me to live free, and live an abundant life.

I started to read my Bible more, and not just read it as though it were a novel, but I began to read it and apply it to my life, as though Jesus were speaking directly to me. I started to increase my belief and faith in what He said in His Word about those He loves, who accept and follow Him. I grew stronger through the Word of God, and through prayer. I started to get a greater revelation of who I was in Christ, and I realized that my identity and worth were not tied up in how people perceived me, or in whether they liked or disliked me. I understood that my identity, and the source of my strength, came completely from Jesus Christ. That revelation revolutionized my life. I started to believe that nothing was impossible for me, and no matter what circumstance came against me, I knew I would get through it, and come through even more powerful, because I have Jesus.

I wasted a lot of time and energy putting my value and self-worth in the hands of other people. Allowing their words and actions towards me to set the standard of how important or unimportant I was. I knew the agony of waiting for and expecting a pat on the back, a congratulations, or a word of encouragement or belief in what I was doing, and felt the disappointment of not receiving it. I would experience hurt when certain individuals in my life would give tons of love and support to others, but would be indifferent or ignore what I was doing all together. This stuff hurt me. I wish it didn't, but it did.

There were times when I would write social media posts and do videos from a place of pain, trying to sound and be strong, while feeling defeated on the inside. Thank God for my late husband, Ian. He was the only one I really trusted to share my deep thoughts and struggles with. He never laughed at me, never judged me, nor did his opinion of me ever change. He knew that I was a strong woman who had battles with my own insecurities and mindset like everyone else. Ian would encourage me, validate me, and push me to continue on. He was my biggest supporter and fan. You can imagine how devastating it was for me to lose someone so significant in my life.

One day during my quiet time with God, I came face to face with the truth that I would not make it to the next level while allowing the opinions of other people to hold so much weight and value in my life. I literally heard that still, small voice of God saying that this was the one thing that had been delaying me and holding me back. Until I received a breakthrough in my thought life, I would not be ready for the next level. God began to minister to my heart and point out to me that if I can't handle the indifference, dislikes, and criticism on this level, how will I survive it on a larger scale? He plainly shared with me that

I wouldn't survive, and I would be eaten alive. I needed time to cultivate, heal, and grow in this area.

I used to always wonder why the same scenario would continue to come up—different environment and different people but the same issue. I began to understand that the common denominator was me. I had to learn to respond differently; otherwise, it would continue to show up in my life. So I had to learn, and boy, was I tested along the way. There were several different occasions where I experienced individuals giving me dirty looks, ignoring me when I greeted them, and showing a lack of enthusiasm as I shared about my milestones and the events in my life. I switched my response. Normally, I would let the behaviours of others hijack my entire day. I would talk about it and play it over in my mind, like a bad movie. Not this time. I was determined to become stronger in my mind, and stronger in my emotions.

I did the opposite of what I would normally do. Instead of avoiding people that weren't the nicest to me, I would intentionally greet them with a hello, and a hug in some cases. I decided that I was not going to change who I was because someone else was acting in a way that was not great. I later understood that everyone is walking around with their own issues and problems, and more times than not, it has nothing to do with us. Over the years, my mistake was that I made it about me. I attached their negativity to me, and created a faulty narrative. Now when people are in their feelings and presenting hot one day and cold the next, I don't take it on. I've learned to meet people where they are at, and to accept their limitations. I've also learned to detach myself from the negativity and not allow it to become a part of who I am and how I show up in the world.

I refer to my default setting because what I noticed was that when the same people that I had a negative experience with historically would come up, I would automatically go to the feeling associated with them, and the history that wasn't positive. I remember having moments when I would catch myself and remind myself that I've let that go, that those are no longer my thoughts towards the individual. The challenge was that I had become so conditioned in this response that it would automatically come up for me. I had to be more intentional. I had to change my default setting. Instead of a negative narrative, I would switch my mindset to something positive and true. I would focus my mind on great qualities about specific individuals, so that my attitude and interactions with them would remain positive.

I understand that just because my default settings towards people have changed for the better doesn't mean we have to become confidants and best friends. All it means is that this negative mindset no longer has a hold on me. That default setting was like a noose around my neck. It drained my energy and limited me from being the best I could be. When around these people, I would usually shrink and dim my light, thinking that this would make them feel comfortable. It was bogus; and the moment I realized that, I got free. I started to love and accept myself better. I became comfortable with the fact that I didn't have to win over everyone. Everyone does not have to like me, cheer me on, or validate what I am doing for me to fulfil my purpose and destiny. God gave me my purpose, and I'm accountable to Him to do what He has created me to do.

This breakthrough within my mind freed me in a powerful way. I have been wanting this freedom for a long time. It was the moment I decided to be more intentional about my thought life that things began to change. I'm not led by my emotions or by the behaviours and attitudes of others; rather, I'm led by the Spirit of God and His Word. Writing out these truths and sharing about these things that I have kept hidden has been the most therapeutic thing for me. Exposing the lies, and putting out there some of the struggles I have had, has taken the power away from these issues. It has removed the shame that I have felt. My secret, silent battle. I had to learn how to take off the mask. I am taking off the mask for people to understand that I am far from perfect. I have my own struggles, just like anyone else. However, I refuse to waste one more day losing in this area. I have never felt so free in my life.

One of the other motivating factors that caused me to really work on my mindset was the unexpected death of my husband. It rocked me to the core. It made me look at my life through a different lens. I realized that I could take nothing for granted. I couldn't just let faulty feelings and thoughts fester within me. I realized that I had to be free every day. If I caused offense, or had been offended, I was more motivated to make it right immediately. I didn't want to wait or delay. My life has changed, in that there is a sense of urgency to fulfill the will of God in my life and do what He has created me to do. In addition, there is a sense of urgency to not hold back, and to be intentional about cultivating real relationships with the right people.

Ian's death changed me in such a powerful way that I could never return to being the same, again. My perspective has changed. I examine everything through one question: "How important is this in light of eternity?" I think beyond this present moment, and I'm constantly motivated by life beyond this life on Earth. I understand fully that only what I do for Jesus Christ lasts. So I pick my battles. I choose to not get easily offended. I let go of things quicker. I focus less on things that are temporal, and focus more on the things that are eternal. I really don't know how someone could walk through what I have, losing my husband the way I did, and be the same. It's impossible for me. I'm not ashamed to say sorry, to admit when I'm wrong, and to have more courageous conversations, for the sake of peace. Life is too short to hold grudges and let misunderstandings linger. I will always have to be intentional about my thought life and the things I meditate on. It's not something that I can do once and never have to do again. In fact, I have to renew my mind daily and pray for the mind of Christ, to think on things that are good, trustworthy, and of a good report. We naturally default to a negative thought or explanation. So it takes work and effort to combat that. Give people the benefit of the doubt, and start from a good place.

There are some powerful things that I have learned from my experience with my thought life and developing a strong mind that I want to share with you:

We have control over our thought life: It is very easy for us to go straight to negative thoughts, and those thoughts impact our behaviour and how we show up in our lives. Random and idle thoughts are dangerous. It's important to be intentional with what we think about and meditate on. More times than not, the negative narrative we have formed is not based on fact. The longer we allow it to linger is the more damage it creates.

Renew your mind daily: It is a biblical principle to daily renew our thoughts. We battle with our own negative thoughts, Satan's attacks on our mind, as well as the words of others that may not be positive. It's imperative that we renew our mind daily. I use the Word of God. Others may use positive affirmations or statements of gratitude to set their mindset right daily.

One of the things I have been learning about is declarations, and making declarations based on the Word of God and His promises concerning my life. Making declarations empowers me to walk in power and truth.

Detach yourself from the negativity of others: For a long time, I made the issues that people had become my issue. I would lose my peace, being worried about why someone was acting weird towards me, trying to figure out what I might have done to warrant this hot and cold response and attitude. I've learned that, oftentimes, how someone is behaving has nothing to do with you, especially if you know that you have not done anything to warrant the negative behaviour. Focus on the facts. Focus on being you. Limit your time with negative people. I've found that if you continue to show up as the positive and friendly person that you are, eventually people will improve in their attitude. You may later learn, without even having to ask, that they were going through their own stuff and, for whatever reason, you triggered them, and they took it out on you. I have more empathy for people who behave this way, because I realize there are other underlying things happening for them. It only leads me to pray for them more.

Your mind controls what your body does: Our ability to think is powerful. When it's healthy, the mind can empower us to do spectacular things with our physical body. It can also cause us to do extraordinary things in our lives. When your mind is strong, you can beat the odds, and there are no limits to what you can do. It's imperative to cultivate a strong mindset daily. Pay attention to the people you allow to speak into your life. Guard what you listen to, specifically as it pertains to media and social media. Fill your mind with the Word of God and positive affirmations that will develop a stronger mind.

Change your default setting: If you have been someone who has always drawn negative conclusions, and it has resulted in your being unhappy, then it's time to change that habit. Become more self-aware. Challenge the thoughts that come to your mind that don't serve you. If you feel as though the behaviour or actions of someone else merit a conversation, then having a courageous conversation could help you have peace and possibly improve the relationship with that individual.

Have more courageous conversations: Over the years, when I've felt hurt, let down, or disappointed, I didn't communicate that. I just kept it moving, instead of dealing with the issues within specific relationships. I have learned the importance of not allowing things to fester, because you can deal with this stuff for years, and it's needless pain. Courageous conversations involve having the difficult conversations that are not comfortable to have but are necessary. It's you initiating a conversation with someone that addresses something they have said or done that has upset you. It even involves addressing your own behaviour and attitude towards someone else, and making it right. When we have these courageous conversations, it allows us to take back the power and peace that was taken from us when we allowed negativity to be the leading force in our lives.

Make time to meditate: Since the death of my husband, I have come to find comfort in times of quietness and solitude. Spending time on your own to pray, think, and meditate, without distractions and interruptions, is powerful. I have found clarity and focus during these quiet times. My self-talk is refined, and what would have normally disempowered me no longer has that hold or control. Examine your thought life. What are you meditating on? Does it serve you and others? If the answer is no, then it requires effort from you to change what you meditate and focus your thoughts on. My go-to is the Word of God. It develops a strong mindset, but it also develops a stronger spirit within me. It causes me to be humbler, and to have more empathy.

Forgive yourself and forgive others: Forgiveness is powerful. I have always been taught that forgiveness is not about the other person, but about you. Forgiveness frees you. I had to forgive myself for the way I treated myself with negative self-talk and negative attitudes and feelings. I had to forgive myself for allowing that negativity to change and impact the way I showed up in life. I had to give myself grace for all the time and energy I wasted over the years, feeling bad about what others have said and done to me. Then I had to forgive others. There are times when people do things unintentionally; other times, it is intentional. Sometimes people don't even understand why they behave the way they do. I've learned to develop more grace, and empathy towards others. It's a process. At times, I get annoyed and frustrated that this stuff keeps coming up with the same people, over the same stuff. However, I've learned to give it over to Jesus Christ. In doing so, I've increased my peace of mind. It is not our job to change people. It is the person's job to do the work necessary to create change within themselves.

Make time to pray: I've always known that praying to God was powerful. The bigger the challenge that is set before me, the more time I need to spend in prayer. Your power is developed during your prayer time and communication with God. Pray the Word of God and speak it out loud. After praying the Word of God and declaring what is true, we have to take action and live it out. Give yourself grace to grow in this. You won't always get it right, and there will be times when you don't win the battle that day. The following day is a new day and a new opportunity to win the battle of the mind. Once that self-awareness has come to your attention, it's impossible to ignore it, and the motivation to grow in developing a strong mind only grows.

Digest content that will develop your faith and mind: What has been extremely helpful in my own healing and development in this area is reading books and listening to powerful sermons. These resources have caused me to see my own experiences of loss from a different perspective. I've learned to reframe my language in a way that is more empowering through the words I read and listen to. There have been powerful sermons from my pastors and other leaders that have really spoken to me. It's the same for the books I have been reading. The devotional book by T.D. Jakes on *Crushing* was very powerful in helping me set the right mindset to start my day. The Word of God continues to build my faith. The examples of the characters in the Bible always help me put things into perspective. I realize that God has always been with them through every difficult season and has always brought them through it. Their stories have built my faith tremendously. Don't remove yourself from the contents of what you read and listen to; rather, put yourself in the role of the character, as if it's being spoken to you directly. Doing so has helped me to grow stronger in my thought life and faith.

THE ROAD TO SELF-DISCOVERY

I 'm now in a peculiar stage in my life. As I've entered a new decade and I'm about to start my journey through my forties, I'm faced with learning about myself in a deeper way, as well as adjusting to a new normal. After everything was settled with my husband's estate, I was left with the question, "Who are you now?" I've always considered myself to be a strong and independent woman. However, a part of me died with the loss of my husband. That place of security was gone. I didn't have the luxury of sharing my struggles with him, brainstorming ideas with him, receiving his constructive criticism. It was all gone when he left this earth.

A lot of who I've become, over the twelve years of our being together, is a result of our marriage and the relationship we shared. I started to develop a greater understanding of myself and my capacity for other things, entrepreneurship being one of them. It was a door that my husband opened to me, and encouraged me to pursue. A lot of my identity was wrapped into my marriage. My husband and I were very close; if you saw one, you would see the other. We did things together, and enjoyed each other's company.

By October 2019, everything had been settled, and now I had the daunting task of figuring out my next steps, thinking about what my life would look like moving forward. My entire world got turned upside down when my husband died. Everything that was normal to me had changed. This radical change was not something I initiated; it took place beyond my control. From his death to settling his estate to selling our matrimonial home and relocating to a new city, so much changed in such a short amount of time that had it not been for the grace of God, I would have lost my mind.

As 2019 was coming to a close, I had some moments of anxiety about entering 2020. It was mixed with excitement, fear, and uncertainty about what would happen to me. It was as though I was discovering life for myself, all over again. I've been used to having my husband for ten years, travelling and doing life together. Now I faced the prospect of having to travel alone, and doing things for myself that I would normally look to my husband to do. It's been a huge transition for me, and I would be lying if I said it was an easy process. I have been learning to give myself grace in this season to learn and grow in the areas that don't come naturally to me. I've also had to work on myself, to develop the courage to do things that are new, and to be okay with having to do them alone, when there are no other options.

The prospect of having to travel alone to celebrate my birthday made me feel uncomfortable. I had some folks in mind that I wanted to travel with me, but I also knew that there was a possibility that they would not be able to join me. I had to make the decision to go anyway and confront every fear I had. Just because I have never done it before alone doesn't mean I shouldn't try. Two years ago, when my husband was still alive, the plan was that he would throw me a big fortieth birthday party. However, as time passed, the desire for that became less, particularly after his death. I realized that I would enjoy travelling and celebrating somewhere warm, instead of having a birthday celebration.

The last ten years have not been an easy journey. They have been filled with loss and ups and downs. As I approach forty, I feel a sense of excitement and anticipation to start this new chapter. It feels as if the sky is the limit to what I can accomplish. Many view getting older as a bad thing, and perhaps have thoughts like, "I'm forty. It is too late to start something new." My perspective is very different. It's never too late to do anything you desire to do. I look at entering my forties as a new adventure, and I look forward to what I will learn and experience as I navigate this new life as a single woman.

One of the things I have discovered in this process is how much I value quiet time and solitude. Naturally, I have a very outgoing, passionate personality. I enjoy engaging with people in conversation and laughter. I'm not intimated by groups, big or small. That being said, I absolutely love those moments when I can step away from it all and be by myself. It's in those quiet moments that I get downloads from God into my heart. New ideas, innovations, and creations come to mind, concerning business and ministry. It's in those quiet moments alone that I experience incredible peace and tranquility. I have discovered that I'm comfortable with my own company. I don't feel lonely in those moments. My thoughts occupy me. I write, read, listen to sermons, watch a family movie on Netflix, and I'm content.

People didn't understand how I was able to remain in my matrimonial home after my husband's death, and remain there alone. I discovered, during that time, that times of solitude and quiet were my best times. As much as I appreciated the guests, there was something wonderful about being alone. I could just be. I didn't have to talk. I didn't have to be engaging or funny.

I could just take off the mask, lay back, and be. In those moments, I experienced much peace that surpasses my own understanding.

I've also discovered my intolerance for negativity in my life. There are a lot of things that I put up with over the years. I did so because I didn't want to hurt people's feelings, but also because I was a people pleaser. I would accept every invitation, and go to events that I didn't really want to attend. I would hang out with people whose company I didn't really enjoy. One of the things that I have gained in this self-discovery is the power of saying no. I do this without apology and without guilt. I have no desire to just do things simply for the sake of doing them. I've embraced living a life that is intentional, and it involves controlling who I give my time to.

It's the worst thing when you keep giving your time away to folks who don't appreciate or value it. I did that for far too long in my life, and I always regretted it. I would leave the company of people feeling drained and unhappy. I made a decision, at the end of 2017, that I would spend time in spaces where I am celebrated and not just tolerated. I continued to commit myself to that, and the resolve has only grown stronger since the death of my husband. Life and time are short, and if I plan to spend time with someone, there must be value exchanged; otherwise, I won't do it. It's important to protect your time and energy at all costs. I believe what also shifted for me was the value I put on my own self-worth. For years, I struggled with allowing others to determine my value, and that impacted how I showed up in life. I've since taken back that power. I've received such incredible clarity about who I am and who God has created me to be that I now live life more focused and more powerful.

In this season, I have also discovered that I don't have a desire to remarry. I've learned how to be content in whatever state I am in. I was married to an incredible man, until the Lord saw it fit to take him home. I've learned that my source of strength and happiness was never about having a husband, children, or a great career. My source of strength and happiness is rooted in Jesus Christ. At the end of the day, when all those things were taken or didn't materialize the way I thought they would, what was always there and what has remained is my relationship with Jesus. There is a strong urgency to serve others that has formed within me; an urgency to make my time on Earth count.

I've learned that my priorities have changed. I'm not driven by money; now more than ever before, I am driven by impact. That is why I share my story. It's my hope that someone will be impacted and empowered to use their experiences of pain and turn them into power, in order to bring about transformation in their own lives. The lives we desire don't just fall into our laps. There is an active role that we each must play in walking out our destiny. God will always speak, and it will be followed up with an action of faith that we must take in order to see the manifestation of His Word and promise.

Developing new and more meaningful connections has become more important to me in this stage of my life. I realize how important it is to be surrounded by the right people—people who will speak faith into your life; people who are creating success; people who, instead of telling you all the reasons why you can't accomplish something, will give you the strategies and the blueprint on how it can be done. I realize how necessary it has been for me to expand my circle and learn from others doing the very thing I want to do, and are successful doing it.

It can be a lonely place when you don't have others who are speaking the same language of desiring more for themselves than what they are currently experiencing. Everyone has to find their own path. However, I find it invigorating and exciting to be in environments where others are working hard towards their dreams. I feed off of that energy, and I get busy for myself as well. My desire is to be a producer and not just a consumer. I take the mandate God has given to us from the beginning of creation, to create, multiply, and have dominion on Earth, very seriously.

On this journey, I'm learning about the power God has given to us who put our trust in Him and follow Him. I don't have to accept what life throws my way. God has the final say, and I strongly believe that no one can prevent us from receiving what God has for us. I didn't know how I was going to get through the loss of my husband and everything that came afterwards. However, when I saw God walk me through it, and I didn't fall apart but kept getting stronger, it was in that moment that I realized that I was unstoppable with Christ in my life. I realized that if I could walk through one of the darkest seasons of my life and not lose my mind, then I could stay the course and fulfil my purpose in this life.

Radical and transformative faith has developed in me, and it cannot be easily broken. The death of my husband should have been the thing to take me out, but it didn't. I'm still here, stronger, more focused, and more powerful than I have ever been in my entire life. The only way that I can explain it is through the encounter I've had with Jesus Christ during this entire ordeal. He has literally transformed my life, and has healed me on many levels. I thought the worst was dealing with my husband's death and his estate. However, it was the revelation of the things in me that needed to change that created a shift that was long overdue and desperately needed.

I've also discovered some of my natural gifts and strengths that I have taken for granted, and have never really paid attention to. One of the questions many struggle with concerns their purpose—what are they on this earth to do? It has become very clear to me that the signs of what we are supposed to be doing have always been present, as early as our childhood. When I really took the time to think about it, I realized that I've always been a writer since childhood. I've always written poems, and did extremely well in English classes in school. In addition, I've always been a communicator and an active listener. I can trace back over the years all the times I've spoken or have been selected to be the spokesperson for a group. I talked in front of groups of people with ease. The signs have always been there. We often overthink our purpose, which results in either remaining stuck or doing nothing. Recently, I've become more aware of my strengths in administration and organization. I never looked at it as a skillset or an asset. It makes me wonder how many people are walking around with many gifts and talents but are disregarding them as nothing special.

The conversation about money is generally an uncomfortable conversation for people. Mainly because there are a number of households living paycheque to paycheque, worrying about mounting debt that they are struggling to pay off. It's stressful, and I remember living that misery for a very long time. This experience has changed the way I think about money, and how I talk about it. Money no longer has power over me, I have power over it. God has given us the power to create wealth. There are many ideas that God has downloaded to us, but we often just make excuses for why they can't work. The root of our excuses is actually fear. If you were to take a pen and brainstorm all the things you are interested in and have the natural skill or talent to do that adds value to someone else, and that people would be willing to pay for, you would be surprised at the wealth you could create. It's about thinking outside-of-the-box and stepping out in faith.

Once you get delivered from wanting to please people all the time, and caring so heavily about what others say or do, you will discover a greater freedom and enjoyment in living your life. You will make a lot of new self-discoveries. I believe it's about embracing the journey and allowing God to develop you along the way. Here are some things to ponder:

Make time for self-examination: Our lives are generally very busy and full with all the things we need to do and all the people that are counting on us to perform certain tasks. In order to show up as your best self, it's important to understand who you truly are. What are the things that make you tick? Embracing self-discovery only creates a better you.

Don't be afraid to try new things: There can sometimes be hesitation in trying something new for the first time. However, give yourself grace as you figure things out and explore a new adventure. There is a whole world waiting for us to explore. Sometimes we stay in the same place for predictability and the sense of familiarity. The challenge with that is we end up being stagnant. Keep things fresh by trying new things, big and small.

Self-discovery takes you out of your comfort zone: As we learn more about ourselves and see certain things that need to change, changing will require us to take action in an area that may not feel comfortable. I strongly encourage you to do it anyway; that's where growth takes place. You will also find that some areas that you felt you were weak in were actually areas of strength. You may have never exercised that muscle to recognize the capacity you had in a specific skillset or talent. We don't know until we try and step out of the mundane and become open to newness.

Expand your network: I personally used to dislike networking events, small talk, and fake people. Now I'm understanding the value of expanding your network and connecting with people in industries that are of interest to you. These are connections that can produce collaborations, new learning and educational opportunities, and a circle of people that will support you and cheer you on as you create and fulfill your dreams. If we are all on the same level, no one can help the other. It's important to invest time, and sometimes money, in environments where you can network and meet people who are doing things you desire to do but haven't had the support or education to do.

Have fun and embrace the journey: Everything always comes down to perspective. Instead of thinking about how much farther you have to go to reach your goals, focus on how much you have grown, and how far you have already come. Look at each experience and stage along the way as a learning experience. Always ask what you can learn from whatever you are going through in life. There are lessons in almost everything that can be of value, not only to you but also to others. Don't take yourself so seriously all the time. Loosen up and laugh more. Laughter is contagious, and it's the way that I alleviate stress. I look for ways to lighten the mood with humour. See this journey as a marathon, and not a sprint. I know we live in a society where we want everything at microwave-speed. However, there is some value in understanding that quality takes time. Building something of significance takes time. So learn as you go, and embrace every second of it.

Be willing to travel the road less travelled: It's not easy to go against the grain and to do things that, perhaps, your friends and family aren't doing. It's not easy to be challenged and questioned about what you are doing because they don't understand it. It can be a lonely place at times. However, when it's something that sticks on you like glue, you wake up thinking about it. You go to bed with it on your mind. Throughout the day, you get downloads of ideas and actions you can take. Destiny will call you, even if the majority doesn't get it or agree. I've learned that my first responsibility is to God, and being obedient to what He has put in my hands to do.

Be clear about your purpose: Having clarity about your purpose is a game changer. Instead of going from person to person, trying to find out what others think about you, and changing with every commentary you get, you become more focused on what you are supposed to be doing. Once you get that clarity, more steps get revealed. You stop looking to people to tell you who you are, and you simply become the person that is aligned with who God designed you to be. You waste less time when you have clarity and focus. I would recommend minimizing how many voices you listen to, as that could add unneeded confusion to your journey.

Check your motives: This is a big one that often gets overlooked. What's your motive for being on this journey? The motive will dictate how far you go on this journey. When your motives are pure, there are no limits to where you will go and what you will do.

Feel the fear, and do it anyway: The growth process is rarely a comfortable one. Sometimes you have to stop talking the death out of something and just go do the thing. Start the business, write the book, speak on stage, tell the person how you feel, apply for the promotion. Just do it. I've learned that we will never know the outcome unless we try. So what if it doesn't work out the way you had hoped or planned? At least you tried. Take chances, if you are serious about living the abundant life that Jesus has intended for you to live. Remember that God is always with you, and there is no need to be afraid.

NO MORE RUNNING FROM THE CALL

I was eight years old when I made the decision that I wanted to be baptized. I understood that accepting Jesus as my Lord and Saviour would lead me to Heaven. Shortly afterwards, in that same year, I received the gift of the Holy Spirit. In those early years, I didn't understand anything about gifts and calling. All I knew was that I loved Jesus, and I knew He loved me. There was something different about me. It wasn't something I planned, nor was it something I asked for or desired. However, the moment I accepted Jesus into my heart and made the decision to follow Him, my life was changed.

I would get up to speak and share a testimony, and the powerful anointing would fall on me each time. I was literally a firecracker. Those around me, particularly the adults, noticed this difference about me, and would encourage me and call me a "little missionary," and later on a "little evangelist." When I heard these things, I was mindful not to let them get to my head. So I would downplay them. Of course, I would give God glory for using me to be a blessing to the people listening. However, I never openly acknowledged myself as a preacher, evangelist, or even a speaker. In fact, I tried to downplay this part of myself. Being different didn't make me popular; in fact, it was a lonely place. At times, I wished that I didn't stand out the way

I did, but each time I shrunk back, the anointing and gift God gave me wouldn't allow me to stay quiet.

I'm very thankful to my pastor at the time, who recognized the gift and started to cultivate it by calling on me to speak. Even though I was speaking for different youth services, as well as main services on Sunday, I still didn't see myself as a preacher or speaker. I saw myself as someone who served, and that if asked to do something, I would do it. Whether that was singing in the choir, directing the children's choir, or helping to clean the church on a Saturday. I saw it all as the same thing—serving God.

I wasn't confident in the gift, and I ran from it, because I felt there was a correlation between being misunderstood and standing out from the younger people in the church. I didn't want the young people to think that I felt as though I was better than them. I didn't seek the attention, nor did I desire it. However, the attention naturally came, just by being myself and letting God use me. Over the years, there were countless men and women who spoke to me about the gifts and the calling that was on my life to travel the world and minister to others. I felt humbled that God would want to use me, and, at the same time, I didn't feel worthy of the call.

Now that I'm older, I realize that Satan has been trying to silence me throughout my life. I was always critical of myself. I let the words of others impact my behaviour. I've always been a very loud, passionate, and fiery speaker, yet I would try to be quieter and try to change my delivery, thinking, perhaps, that would make people receive me better. That was never the case. When people decide to not like you, they don't need many reasons for the sentiment. As I trace my life from the beginning, I realize that the woman you see today has always been the person that God created me to be. I've always been social, outgoing, and friendly. I've always been a writer and a communicator. However, I wasted a lot of time trying to hide those gifts, thinking that would get me acceptance, and that, somehow, I would feel less different. It didn't work.

I went through a season of frustration, because I knew God had called me to more. I also knew that there had to be more to my experience with God than what I was experiencing at my local church. So after twenty-six years of being in the same local church, God spoke to me about transitioning and joining another minister who was starting a church. Shortly after leaving and starting this ministry, God brought my husband into my life. I strongly believe that God used Ian to help me to truly understand who God has called me to be. He stretched my belief systems, and he opened my understanding of the supernatural—healing, miracles, and unlocking gifts—that I never really thought about.

Once married, my husband and I joined the same congregation. It was very different from what I was used to. I learned a lot there, and felt as if I grew as a leader. However, I still was not walking in my calling. Now I was in a place that caused me to water down myself even more. I knew deep down that there was more. However, I stayed, for the sake of comfort. I was busy in ministry, doing all the church activities, to the point where it felt like a second job. The challenge was that I was not growing spiritually. I was concerned about the lack of spiritual growth, and, at the same time, uncertain about how to grow, since I was in an environment that wasn't going to teach me or mentor me in my gifts. So I resolved that it was no big deal. I would carry on and accept just being mundane and ordinary.

As time went on, God began to minister to my husband about the need for a change, as he also craved for more of God and believed that there was more to our walk with God than what we were doing. He had the conviction that it was time to leave. I didn't believe in hopping from church to church. I liked stability, and was concerned about where else we would go to serve. I remember our spiritual mentor telling Ian that before we could leave, God would speak to me first. I sighed a sigh of relief, because I knew God hadn't spoken to me about leaving, so I figured we would just stay put and that would be the end of it. Not so. Shortly after that meeting with our spiritual mentor, God began to speak to me and share that it was time. One thing Ian and I were certain of was that we were called to marketplace ministry. We believed strongly that the marketplace needed not only our skillsets, but also the gospel of Jesus Christ. We understood that our ministry would not look the traditional way that everyone expected. We would not be pastors leading a mega church. We were called to reach the unchurched, and it may be unorthodox and out-of-the-box for religious folks, but this was what we believed God was calling us to do.

My husband and I stepped out in faith. We didn't see any other church locally that was doing what was in our heart to do. We feared that joining another church similar to where we were coming from would cause us to fall back into the same routine—being busy, but not growing. So for six years, we did a home church, with big dreams of reaching the unchurched for Jesus Christ. The challenge was that we needed more cultivation and support from a mentor to walk this out. What essentially happened was the opposite of what we wanted to accomplish. If I felt watered down before, it intensified even more during this time of worshipping in a home church. It made us complacent, too comfortable, and relaxed. It was a very uncomfortable place to be in. I often questioned myself, "What are we really doing? Whose lives are we impacting?"

The big shift that took place for us was when Apostle Bible Davids and his wife, Prophetess Rebecca Bible-Davids, came to town. They arrived in Toronto in December 2017 and hosted an event. They have a powerful supernatural and prophetic ministry. So Ian and I started to attend the services. If I am to be honest, both Ian and I had our guards up. We weren't interested in being rolled back into traditional church. We had spent our lives serving in ministry, as we both grew up in church. We knew that we were gifted and that most pastors and leaders looked at us with ideas of how they could plug us into their ministry. We weren't interested in what we had always done. Ian and I sincerely wanted to do the will of God.

Therefore, we would casually attend services, but we would not commit to becoming members, or serving in ministry. We didn't know where God was taking us, but we immensely enjoyed the ministry of Apostle Bible Davids and his wife, Prophetess Rebecca Bible-Davids. Ian and I brought in the new year of 2018 with Supernatural Life Center Toronto. My hunger for God continued to grow. God started to tug at my heart about becoming a member of Supernatural Life Center. At the time, Ian was not ready for that, and since we were a team, I would not do something that would cause disunity in our marriage. We agreed to continue to pray about it, while attending the services.

It was that summer of 2018 that my husband's health started to significantly decline. It was in those moments that I was grateful that we weren't just doing home church anymore, but that there was a place I could go to pray and be prayed for. I still wasn't at the place to join them as a member, but Ian and I both enjoyed the ministry. I recall the day that my husband died. It was a Sunday. Ian was frequently tired, and often didn't have the energy to get up early to go to church, so I would go alone. I remember it was a powerful service. I called him after service and shared. I remember some of the members asking about Ian, and I encouraged them to pray for my husband, not knowing that by the end of that day my husband would breathe his last breath.

When Ian died, I felt lost. I didn't know who I was or what I was supposed to do now. I didn't fit in where I was coming from, I didn't fit in where I was, and I had not yet arrived at the place where I was supposed to be going. The thought of the things I had to do seemed daunting, and the only peace I got from the chaos of what had become my life was when I slept and when I was in church. I knew that everything in my life had changed and would never be the same, but the one constant was being in church. Not just any church—Supernatural Life Center, under the leadership of Apostle Bible Davids and Prophetess Rebecca Bible-Davids.

Once the funeral was over, I scheduled a meeting with the Apostle and Prophetess, and expressed that I needed their support, and I submitted myself to their leadership and spiritual guidance. I needed that spiritual covering. I had no desire for position or title. I needed a place where I could heal, and where I could discover what God wanted me to do next, and how He would help me navigate the days ahead. I will forever be grateful to my pastors for their care and patience with me during one of the most difficult seasons of my life.

After my husband died, I did not delay in attending the church services that were held at Supernatural Life Center. In fact, I increased my attendance. I was there Wednesday, Friday, and Sunday morning and night. Some thought I was pushing myself too much, that I needed time to grieve. The truth is, I could not just sit around grieving and crying. It was not helpful to me. The only place that brought me refuge and peace was when I was in church, worshipping and having an encounter with God every time. It was during this time that God began to heal my heart, mind, and spirit. Every time God ministered through either Apostle Bible Davids or Prophetess Rebecca Bible-Davids, it was always a word that spoke to where I was. They were words that gave me the tools and strategies, through the Word of God, on how to walk through that season. I learned different ways to see what I was going through. I spent less time feeling sorry for myself, and more time growing in faith and power.

As time went on, I decided to join one of the ministry teams. However, I realized later on that I was still running. I had baggage from my previous assemblies, and it was still impacting me. I avoided the microphone like the plague. I didn't acknowledge the call to speak, and I was quite content to keep away from it. There are some who desire the microphone, and ask for it, but that was not me. The leader of my ministry, who happened to be my sister-in-law, would try to get me to lead in prayer using the microphone, and I would avoid it and stay away. Part of me was still carrying the baggage of the past of not wanting people to think that I just came and already I was taking the microphone. I still battled with the people pleasing and faulty narrative. I also struggled with having a real relationship with the pastors that I served, as I never really had a real relationship with previous pastors. I was used to serving and doing the assignment they gave me, but what I wasn't used to was having my pastors actually care about how I was doing, and invest time in connecting with me, with no other motive other than simply caring. It was an entirely new experience for me that I needed to get used to.

I realized that I had some religious ideas and things that I needed to be set free from. By the time the church transitioned to a new building, I was already being set free from those old mindsets. I had not yet accepted the call to speak, but I was growing in my identity in Christ. I was becoming stronger in my faith. I cared less about the opinions of others, and I was not trying to people please. I was feeling more confident and more powerful. The Word of God was transforming me. My story was not over because my husband died; there was hope. I was determined to keep going. I believed that if I was still alive then there must be something God had for me to do. So I continued to push forward, in spite of all the opposition and challenges I was facing along the way. I sincerely believed that there was another side to my crushing season, and because I believed that, I faced every day with an expectation that God was working out something great for my good. My perspective changed. Though it was hard, and stretched me like nothing before, my perspective changed. My trials weren't punishment, and my life was not over. I would recover. God wasn't through with me yet. God became my true source of strength.

When we transitioned out of our old building, I started to serve, and I stopped running from the microphone. When I was asked to do something that involved being in the front, I stopped running. I began to understand that everything I do is not about me; it's about being in service to others. If God would have me lead a prayer, read a scripture, or speak, then that was what I would do, because it was about giving God glory and serving His people. Once I took myself out of the equation, I was able to drop off those heavy weights of religion and past church experiences that were limiting me and holding me back.

It became clear to me that God had something great for my life, regardless of what I have been through. I started to rediscover my voice. Even my content on social media changed. There was a greater focus on my business and brand being Christ-centred. I needed people to understand that had it not been for Jesus Christ, I would have lost my mind. I moved from leading myself, and building a business with Jesus being an afterthought, to partnering myself with God as my CEO. I became driven by a desire to fulfil my purpose and my assignment that God had given me.

The more I shared my testimony and demonstrated to people the grace of God, the more people were inspired and encouraged as they walked through their own challenging losses and difficult seasons. I realized that though the enemy meant my trial for evil, God meant it for my good. He would use this tragedy to bless every person that He had assigned to the message He had given to me—a message of transformation, radical change, and faith that is developed and cultivated in the fire. I began to understand that I had to walk through this season, and I had to draw my strength from God to show others that have been watching that it's possible. It's possible to go through a horrific loss and come out of it more powerful, more focused, and stronger than ever before. It's possible with God. It doesn't deny the pain and loss I feel at not having my husband by my side. However, it demonstrates how faithful and powerful God is to keep me through the darkest valleys of life.

As I increased my prayer life and the reading of His Word, my identity and purpose became even clearer. I understood that what I was created to do was always evident. However, I let the opinions, behaviours, and words of others cause me to water myself down. That would never happen again, because I knew too much now. Walking through a tragic loss changes you. I have stopped taking things and people for granted. I don't assume I will have another time to do something, so I do it right away.

The powerful thing about this season is the growth and maturity in my mindset and perspective. I have no desire for what others have. Nor do I have a desire to be like others. What I do have a desire for is to be the best version of myself, to show up daily as the person that God has created me to be. I have finally come into alignment with God and His plan for my life, and, as a result, I have never felt freer or more alive than in this moment. What drives me is my love for God, my desire to fulfil the assignment He has given me, and my desire to make the greatest impact on Earth that I can. I want to be effective with the gifts He has given me to share with the world. Things happen when you start to believe what God said about you. When you start to believe that what is written in the Bible is not just for someone else, but also for you. I don't believe in impossibilities; I believe in all things being possible with God. This makes some people uncomfortable, both Christian and non-Christian alike. It's a radical faith. It doesn't make sense and can't be rationalized. I choose to live a supernatural lifestyle. I have more peace and more power, as I submit to God and trust Him to order my steps in every area of my life.

During this part of my self-discovery, I've learned a few things that I hope will help you:

The evidence of your purpose has always been present: Most people spend too much time asking, "What is my purpose?" I've come to learn that it has always been present. I learned that if I traced the timeline of my life, there has always been evidence of my gifts as a writer, a speaker, and a person that loved working with people. Don't overthink it; there are gifts that you naturally possess that have been given for you to use to serve and impact the world around you.

You can't run from who you naturally are: It's not possible to hide who you naturally are; it will come out. When we make it about ourselves, it's rooted in selfishness. Showing up and using your gifts is not about you, it's about serving and impacting the lives of others that will benefit from your skills, talents, and gifts.

When you become clear about your purpose, you don't need a cheering section: For a long time, I didn't feel confident on my own. I felt I needed my husband's affirmation, and the validation of others, in order to take the next step. I felt I needed that security blanket, just in case things didn't work out. God has shown me that once the assignment is clear, my job is to do it. He will align the right people around me that will help me manifest the vision. Whether people affirm or validate it is irrelevant. Spend less time talking to multiple people and hearing various opinions, which leave you more confused. Confusion keeps people stuck. When you know what your main purpose is, the confusion ends. You look to God instead of people. People cheering you on is nice, but it's not a requirement.

Understanding your identity is key to your success: I let others try to define me. I let theirs be the prominent voice. It impacted what I did and how I did it. The voices of people became louder than God's voice. That restricted me, and I was limited in my thinking and capacity as a result. When I came into alignment with the truth of my identity in Christ and believed it for myself, I stopped holding back. I broke free from the yokes around my neck that were bringing me down. I released people. I stopped comparing myself to others. I understood that there was no competition; there was only one me, which meant I was unique. I embraced who God made me to be, and found contentment, peace, joy, and power. People's shade and indifference towards me had little effect. In fact, at times I would laugh. The enemy of my soul was not going to defeat me in this area and waste more of my time. Identity crisis is a real thing, and as long as your identity is not firm and clear to you, it is left up to anyone to label you and box you in.

Support will come from surprising places: Sometimes the people to support you and have your back turn out to be people that you may not have known that long, but they believe in you and your mission. Sometimes we have to lower our expectations of those individuals in our lives that should be there for us more but aren't. I had to learn to lower my expectations, and I'm happier as a result. I get the limitations of those individuals, and I know not to look to them for what I need. You can still love those individuals, but know that they aren't the ones that you can lean on when you need support.

If God has called you to it, He has given you the capacity for it: Our minds are so limited. God knows exactly what He is doing when He calls us to do something. He has already seen our future. When we grasp that revelation, we will stop worrying about money, sickness, and world problems. We will put our confidence in God and His plan for our lives and what He has for us to do in order to be a part of the solution to problems. Jesus and His disciples brought solutions; they didn't add problems. He called you for a reason, and you are uniquely designed by God for the assignment He has called you for. That's why there is no need for comparison. I don't want what others have; I want what God has for me. That change in perspective will free you and lift the weight of comparison, competition, and jealousy off of you.

BECOMING

I grew up in a very loving home, with wonderful parents and a great brother. I consider myself blessed for those wonderful experiences within my upbringing. I used to think that so much time was wasted struggling with my mindset, people pleasing, and limiting myself because of my own limiting beliefs, as well as others'. I've come to a place in my journey where I have a heart of gratitude for everything that I have been through, because it has brought me to this moment. Every experience, whether good or bad, has contributed to the woman I have become and the woman that I am becoming.

On this journey, I've become a person who has learned to create boundaries. I've learned that it's okay to say no and not be available to everyone. I recognize the importance of self-care. I realize that if my tank is empty and depleted, then I have nothing to pour out, and I will be ineffective and unhelpful to those I am here to serve. I've learned to not allow manipulation and guilt trips to be the driving force to get me to do something. It's been a journey, but I feel stronger since learning how to protect my time, understand myself better, and do the work to improve.

For the first time in my life, I feel comfortable in my own skin. I don't feel a need to keep up with what other people are doing. I have no desire to compare or to be jealous of what others are doing and what they have. I feel confident in staying in my own lane. I embrace the process and journey with all the highs and lows that come with it. Instead of complaining or being frustrated and upset, I look at the lessons to be learned in every situation I am facing. I think about how I can have more courageous conversations, in an attempt to help others grow as well. Fear is not the thing that drives me, faith does.

I've become a person that has learned how to trust God fully. I've learned that my faith in Jesus Christ is real. When I drew closer to God, I learned more about who He is, and in learning more about who He is, I learned more about who I am. The voices of others have gotten smaller and quieter, and the voice of God has gotten louder, to the point where it dominates my spirit. He has given me a peace that surpasses my understanding. I understand now that I had to walk through these various trials of life to prepare me for this moment in time.

Through personal development, I have learned that I can determine who I will be and how I show up in the world. I decide what type of experience I want people to have when they interact with me. For so long I've craved acceptance from others, and I've come to realize that what was missing was my acceptance of myself. God has demonstrated His love to me by sending His Son. The magnitude of His love for me was displayed during His care of me through the loss of my husband. I've come out on the other side of that trauma, and I'm better having gone through it. I didn't turn to substances. I didn't shrink away. Instead, I turned, with open arms, to Jesus.

I've learned that the most important opinion is the Lord's and whether He is pleased with me and the things that I'm doing. He has become the centre of my world. I understand that it doesn't make sense for me to do all these things in His name, only to have Him say in the end that He is not pleased and that I must live separate from Him for all eternity. I had to learn to submit myself to His perfect will, even when it made my flesh feel uncomfortable. Even when the process hurts, I've learned to trust Him anyway. I've seen the outcome and the other side of darkness. It's light, love, peace, and freedom.

This journey has changed my perspective of the world around me. I see it with new eyes. I've learned that there are a lot of hurting people around, and many who do not know how to cope or deal with the things that life throws their way. The pain and trauma are real and can't be neglected. I can't offer a treatment or therapy that was used to get me to this place of peace and restoration. All credit goes completely to Jesus Christ. My faith has deepened as a result. I know that if He could take me through this valley, then He can do the same thing for anyone who believes in Him.

I naturally like to be in control. It is the most uncomfortable thing for me to put full control in the hands of others. I often doubt they can meet my need or operate on a level of excellence to my standard. I tend to want to do things on my own to avoid the frustration of putting my trust in others, only to have them let me down. However, after the death of my husband, the Lord taught me how to let go and trust. The truth is, I had no choice. Everything I needed was in the hands of third parties, and all I could do was pray, be patient, and wait. Not a very easy thing for me to do. God taught me humility in this season of my life. Though the waiting process felt gruelling and draining, I eventually had to come to the realization that if I didn't let go of the things I couldn't control, I would forfeit my peace. I made a decision to take a stand to trust God, and trust that He was working on the other variables and working them out for my good. He came through and exceeded my expectation.

I stopped being afraid to confront the things about myself that I didn't like and that made me feel uncomfortable. I understand the importance of doing self-reflection and putting in the work on yourself in order to improve and be better. I stopped letting myself be measured by the standards of other people, and I started to look to Jesus as my standard. I now extend more grace when working with people. There is an increase in empathy towards others and what they may be going through in their lives that contributes to their behaviour.

I understand my worth, and I enter rooms knowing that God has designed me to be powerful, to have dominion, to multiply, and to increase in all areas of my life. To experience lack in any area of my life is a contradiction of God and His Word. I used to accept this scarcity mindset and way of being. I've come to understand that it's not God's will for us to live in poverty and lack. Jesus came to Earth for us to have life and to have it more abundantly (John 10:10). So I don't accept that my resources needed to build wealth is contingent on a job or an individual person. There is nothing wrong with jobs, but this earth belongs to God, and everything I need comes from Him. I no longer worry about money. I know for many people money, or the lack thereof, consumes their thought life in a negative way. Money is just energy produced in a physical form. We exchange money for a service rendered. It doesn't have power over me. I no longer chase after it. I strongly believe that when we come into alignment with our purpose, we will attract money and wealth.

I've heard the saying that "success loves speed," and that very well may be true. However, I've found that it was more stressful when I was bouncing around, trying different opportunities, trying to turn them into something profitable that would replace my full-time income. It became a desperation, and I was running after it, and I've found that the more we chase money, the farther away from us it gets. It's when I stopped chasing after it, and shifted my motivation and focus, that I started to get positioned stronger in my finances. I embraced the process and the levels to success—the sacrifice, time, discipline, focus, and consistency. Most people want the success but not the work that is required to acquire that success. I have learned that it's one thing to hit a milestone in your business or career, and it's an entirely different thing to sustain it and keep growing to the next level. Sustainable success that has longevity does not happen overnight. Those that are on this journey for the long haul will reap the harvest.

Everyone should not hear what you are doing. I appreciate working quietly behind the scenes. Keep your head down and do the work, and those around you can learn about what you are doing when the finished product is ready. When we tell people what we are doing too prematurely, they will list all the reasons why it is a bad idea, and why we aren't able to do it. What has always surprised me is that the people who say what you are attempting can't be done are usually the people who have never attempted what you are doing. They have no personal experience, other than the stories of third parties. I have learned to ponder things in my heart, pray, and let God lead me to the people that I am to share with, who have the faith and capacity to handle the dream and vision that God has given to me.

The right circle is very important. As I've been going through my own metamorphosis, I realize how important it is to have diverse groups of people around you. People that share similar values and ambitions. Individuals who are creating success, walking in faith, and taking action. Their action matches their talk. I realize that in environments with people like that you get energized and an even greater fire ignites within you to get the work done and to serve the world with what you have to impact their lives.

There are many excuses that we often use to justify why we are living a life that we are not happy with. We'll talk about the challenges of life—trying to balance children, a full-time career, a spouse, school, and all the other things that we fill our time with. I don't negate the fact that it requires work, time, and energy to give of yourself to other people and then try to find the energy and motivation to do something for yourself. However, if the intentional effort is not made to take care of yourself and work towards your own dream, time will pass and you will be sixty-five years old, or older, asking yourself, "Where did the time go? What did I do with my life?" It does not serve you, your family, or your church if you keep delaying walking in your purpose. You do yourself and others a disservice. If your job is a place that is toxic and unfulfilling, find another one. Time is too short to be spending so much time doing the things we do not love.

I've learned that the lifestyle that I desire to live requires sacrifices. The value I used to put in stuff has changed. I've learned the power of leveraging and the importance of having assets of value to leverage. Society puts emphasis and value on stuff, usually stuff that have no value and give no return. Clothes, trips, and cars are all nice, but you receive no return from them. This journey has taught me the importance of investing in things that give you a return. It makes no sense to look like a million bucks, and you have red and minuses in your bank account.

For the ten years that I was working at my corporate job, I was a consumer. I didn't value the money I had, and I wasn't the best steward. I have come to understand the need to stop being a consumer, and to start being a producer. Become the person that produces and creates the innovative products and services that can help serve and offer value. I've always found more joy in giving than in receiving, and that's still the case. It comes down to small changes that can be made in our habits and mindset consistently, over time, that can literally transform our lives. In just twelve months, my life did a total one-hundred-and-eighty-degree turn. I'm becoming the woman I knew I always was, and the woman that my husband always saw when he looked at me. The difference is that I'm not waiting for others to see it or believe it, I believe it for myself. I'm not waiting for people to agree before I take action. I am simply taking action and doing the work.

I'm becoming a woman who is happier, more at peace, focused, and on fire. A woman who is not afraid to take risks and enjoy adventure. I'm becoming less of myself and more like Jesus. He died thousands of years ago, and the impact of His life and death are still being talked about and celebrated. It's my desire to live a life worth living, and to challenge and empower others to do the same. The sacrifice that Jesus Christ made when He died on the Cross cannot be wasted. Every time I am tempted to slow down, or have a pity party, I remember the sacrifice Jesus made for me and the world. I put my big girl pants on, wash my face, and go forward, knowing that He is with me every step of the way.

As I get ready to start this next chapter of my life, many things come across my mind. One word sums it all up: GRATEFUL. I'm grateful for everything that I have endured and overcome. I'm better because of it. Some may think that my life is over—I'm a widow, turning forty, with no children, and no career in the corporate world, with none of the things that society uses to measure success. The truth is, I could have all those things and still not be happy. I have learned how to be content and fulfilled in every stage of life that I am in. I've accepted the fact that I am one who travels on the road less travelled. I am different. I stand out. And I won't do what is traditional and expected of me. Though these things may make some people uncomfortable, they don't make me feel uncomfortable. Every time I tried to live a life that was normal, with no twists and turns, it never happened. I'm not trying to be a follower, nor am I trying to fit in. My focus is on making an impact and being effective in the assignment that God has given me.

On this journey, I've had to examine my motive, and really ask myself, "Why am I doing this? Why do I want to do this?" First, I recognized that I didn't ask for it, but actually ran from it for most of my life. Once I came to that realization, I got to the core of it. My motive comes down to my obedience to the call of God on my life, to do what He has given me to do, so I can be a blessing to the world around me. There is a sense of urgency that I can't shake. I'm convinced, without any doubt, that this is my time to *ignite*, to step into a new level that I have never been before, and to have a greater impact on this world. The motive is not about me; it's about being in service to others.

I've always been an advocate for the underdog, and I always want to see people win. There is a message of hope, resilience, and faith in my story, and it's my prayer that those who read it will not just be inspired, but will also take action and move into their purpose. It's not enough to just be excited and fired up, that excitement needs to be backed up with the work and the action necessary to produce the desired outcomes. I became tired of being a spectator. I started to recognize the gifts that were inside of me that the world could benefit from. I stopped thinking small, and started to dream bigger.

Radical change occurred in my life, and I wasn't prepared for it. I could never have imagined, in a million years, that I would not be growing old with my husband. I had to make a choice to fight back, trust God, and turn my pain into power. I'm on this journey because I want to help others do the same. Tragedy doesn't have to cripple us and take us out; we can recover with the help of God. We can develop resilience, and in the midst of adversity, still inspire others and create something beautiful in a dark season.

I'm becoming the best version of myself, and I couldn't be happier to be on this journey. Undoubtedly, there will be other challenges in life. The confidence I have is that God is with me. If He could see me through the loss of my dad and my husband, not to mention all the financial challenges along the way, I am confident that, no matter what mountains or valleys come my way, God is faithful and He has already created a plan to see me through.

Here are some things I have learned about becoming:

Trials are meant to make you stronger: I wish I could tell you that I understand why we go through the things we go through. Unfortunately, I don't have an answer to that. What I know is that we have to choose how we respond to each trial as it comes. Understand that there is a greater purpose that we may not understand at the time, but it becomes more evident as time goes on.

Life is a marathon, not a sprint: It's taken me nearly forty years to get the breakthroughs that I'm experiencing in my life now. Don't be so quick to run pass each stage. Embrace it, and learn from it. These are the life lessons that will help you develop into the best version of yourself. We can't run from pain; we can't make it go faster. Gain perspective and understanding that you can carry forward to help yourself and others.

Become comfortable in your own skin: Developing a healthy perception and belief in yourself takes consistent work. It doesn't just happen. It requires you to understand that you are loved by God. He has designed you and created you perfectly. Learning to love yourself and all that makes up who you are empowers you to love those around you and in your life better.

You don't need permission to take action: A lot of time gets wasted while you wait for people to validate you and agree with what you are doing. I've learned that we have the capacity to do what God has called us to do. We grow in the process. If we wait to get everyone in agreement with what we are doing, we will never take action.

Listen to that still, small voice: God is always speaking, and sometimes we just have so many other voices speaking at the same time that it drowns out the voice of God. The folks that are speaking to you likely have good intentions, but it adds more confusion when you are listening to too many voices. Get clarity, hear from God, share with a select few that are sound, wise, and have some experience in doing what you are trying to do.

Don't try to convince people of who you are, just be that person: I've come to understand that our family and close friends, as much as we love them, aren't always the best people to see us for who we truly are. There is a level of familiarity that gets in the way of them seeing how gifted, talented, and great we truly are. Don't waste your energy trying to convince them. Focus on the people whom you are called to, and show up each day ready to serve those people. Your family and friends may never see you as that person, and that's okay. They don't have to see you that way for you to live boldly as the person God has designed you to be.

Discover your voice, and use it: Things get left unsaid far too often. Years go by with us feeling hurt, disappointed, and underappreciated. It's a weight and baggage that you don't need. Develop the courage to speak up, to tell someone that you trust and respect when they have crossed the line, or if they have hurt you. Have a voice when you don't agree with something. You can be respectful and still share your thoughts on a situation. Do not allow others to silence you, and do not silence yourself.

Check your motive: Examine your reason behind doing what you are doing. If you are doing it to follow others, or if you are doing it to be popular, then it won't last. There needs to be a strong belief in what you are doing, particularly in the beginning when you are first building. Your resolve has to be so strong that even when there are criticisms and people are not fans of you and your message, it does not deter you from showing up and serving those that you are called to. A strong why and motive is what will push you forward when you are tired or experiencing challenges along the way.

Challenge yourself to always grow: There should always be a self-inventory. I learned from my purpose coach, Nicole O. Salmon, the importance of doing that inventory. I recommend doing it at the end of each week. Do it at the end of the month. Do it at the end of each quarter. How are you doing when it comes to your goals? What are the things that you need to keep? What are the things that you should change? What are some habits that are serving you and your purpose that may need adjusting? Assess your wins and celebrate them.

Fight the imposter syndrome: If you are conditioned to feel as though you don't belong in a certain room, and that others are better than you or smarter than you, it will limit you from progressing forward in your goals. You have something of value to add to the conversation. Your experiences, knowledge, and skills are important. Don't let others judge your value. Know that you have value.

Keep your peace: There are things all around us that threaten to steal our peace. It could be as simple as a bad drive on the highway, a rude cashier at the store, disrespectful children, an insensitive spouse, and the list goes on. Sometimes when things are piling up and you feel like you are going to explode, give yourself a time out. Step away and grab some quiet moments to reflect on all the things that you are grateful for. Look for the positive. Don't allow yourself to be easily frustrated or annoyed. You won't always get it the first time. It's something we have to be intentional about. When you keep your peace, you are happier.

Protect your time: This is another principle that was emphasized even more by my purpose coach, Nicole O. Salmon. If we are not intentional about scheduling self-care days, that time will be booked by someone else trying to make use of our time. Create boundaries, so that you are not spread too thin, and you don't find yourself wasting time doing things that are not productive.

Develop an attitude of gratitude: It is easy to come up with the things that are going wrong. It's even easier to complain. Change your default setting. Instead of being a complainer and spreading more negativity, reframe your language and start to speak positively. Think about the things you can be grateful for. Be specific and say them out loud.

Be the change you want to see: One of the principles I try to live by is being the change I want to see. Lead by example. If you want to change culture, let it start with you. We have the power to make a difference. It only takes one person to shift the attitude of the overall environment.

Be a solution provider: I have learned that we are solution providers. We have a solution to a specific problem or need that the people we are here to serve have. Always think about how you can help. When you have that attitude, it goes beyond just making money. Making the money is a bonus, the real value is in being able to help people solve a problem. The value is in meeting that need and impacting more people.

Never give up: When you make this journey bigger than yourself, it will propel you forward. There will be many things that will come before you to deter you, distract you, or stop you. Stay focused on the assignment God has given you, and stay focused on whom He has called you to serve. People are waiting for you to step into alignment with your purpose, so that they can be ignited in their purpose as well.